COMMUNICATION

from

GOD

Mary Lynn Tao

Communication from God

Editor: Loral Pepoon, Cowriterpro Editorial Services
Cover Art: Emma Slippy
Published by: Selah Press Publishing, LLC, Nashville, TN

ISBN: 978-1-953211-04-0
Printed in the United States of America

Additional copies of *Communication from God* may be purchased on amazon.com. If you would like to reach Mary Lynn Tao, email her at COMMUNICATIONFROMGOD@gmail.com.

CONTENTS

WELCOME, READER!

Communication from God. Don't you love the title of this book? Did you find yourself thinking, *Wait! What??* Was there a part of you that WANTED to believe that some type of communication from or with God might be possible for you? I believe He has put me here to tell you, IT IS!!

I've got some great stories to tell about communication from God. It happens!! I mean, I was whispered to by God, inside my head, to NOT go directly home because the guy in the vehicle behind me was following me!!

Then there was the time I was out of town, staying in a hotel for the night, thinking about my "care group." Our care group met once a week and was comprised of a small number of people from our local congregation. I was thinking about an experience I'd had and was wondering if it would be wise for me to share it or not with the group. I was asking God for direction as I brushed my teeth and got ready for bed. As I bent over the sink, I saw letters around the rim of the drain. A word was looking back at me. I read SPEAKMAN. Coincidence? I thought not. Our God is not limited in ways of getting through to us. Speakman was the brand of faucet the hotel used, but it ALSO happened to be the tool my Lord used to convince me I had information that I needed to speak! So, at our next meeting, I shared my testimony—drain story and all. To my delight, one sister told me that my information had truly come at a very pivotal point for her. God knew. God wanted me to share and got the message through to me. He's creative!

These two stories are just a couple of the many instances that have convinced me that our God WANTS to interact with us. He WANTS us to know He hears, He sees, He loves, and He delivers! I believe He also wants us to share Him and His care for us with others!

Won't you just TRY to read this book? Would you entertain the slightest possibility that God truly loves you? Would you consider that He would really enjoy communicating to you in a way you can understand? This book was written for people just like you. In fact, it was written FOR YOU. Enjoy!

Most sincerely,

Mary Lynn Tao

Mary Lynn Tao

Chapter One

COMMUNICATION FROM GOD— DOES IT STILL HAPPEN?

In the 1978 movie Superman, a green crystal "called" to Clark Kent. He was around eighteen years old, and the crystal, buried beneath the floor of the barn, managed to send some kind of a signal to his Krypton brain. The message was "Come here and get me!" Clark—somehow—knew just what to do after he got the signal: hike up into the tundra region and throw that hunk of telepathy into the wild blue. Being hurled into frigid temperatures, I suppose, caused the crystal to respond by building him his own house complete with a machine that projected holographic images of his real mom and dad (who had anticipated the questions an eighteen-year-old-Krypton-planet boy might have having grown up on planet Earth) and those images *talked to him!*

I'm not from the planet Krypton, but I am an alien. My home is Heaven, and my Father is Creator of the universe. I've been allowed to live here on planet Earth for a little while encased inside a physical body. Someday my physical body will shut down and my spiritual body, the real me, will return to my Father, and I will live with Him.

I cannot remember a time when I wasn't aware of the real me inside this receptacle; nor can I recall ever feeling disconnected from my Father. I never had a green crystal, I simply *knew* He was actively communicating with me. It has been my joy to simply have an awareness of His presence with me always.

And I'm Not Alone!!

The longer I live, and the more people I meet, the more aware I become that there are a host of people just like me: people who feel connected to our Father in a deeply intimate, personal way. They may never have heard His voice nor ever been able to discern that a particular thought was from Him, but they feel wonderfully, comfortably close to Him. They're aware that they're loved, accompanied, and guided even though they may have nothing on which to specifically assert such a claim. They simply have a feeling. They just "know." Then, there is another group: those who feel wonderfully, deeply connected to our Father but who ALSO believe they've been given specific thoughts from Him, heard His voice, dreamed a dream, or seen a vision given specifically by Him to them!

The difficulty I have experienced is that those of us who have experienced a specific intervention or communication from God are often seen as suspect by those who love Him every bit as much as we do, but who have not, to their awareness, received a direct communication from Him. They may be very well aware of blessings, or perhaps talents (hospitality, the gift of teaching or encouraging, leadership, giving, etc.) they have received from Him. But, actual "God shared this with me" communication is foreign to them. If it hasn't happened to them, they reason, then surely, it hasn't happened to anyone else. It couldn't. They read their Bibles. They pray. They love their neighbors and they love God. If He was going to speak to anyone, surely He would speak to them. Surely.

One friend put it simply: "If He talks to you, Mary, why doesn't He talk to me?"

To answer that question let me say, first of all, I can't answer for God. Secondly, I don't know the answer.

As a little girl I was routinely taken to church with the people who raised me—my parents. Sitting in the pew, Sunday after Sunday, I found myself sitting and listening, singing and listening and being "informed" inside my head, not by an audible voice but more like an impression or a thought: *this is good, but there's more—there's so very much more.* I was aware of that thought over and over and over and over.

I developed a love for the people in the congregation, and I knew they loved me and my family as well. Furthermore, I knew that the love we all felt for one another was linked to the love each of us felt for God—and the love we felt coming from Him to us.

Resonating Impressions

Still, we sat and listened and sang and listened and stood and listened. Somehow, during the listening, I heard more than the words of the minister or the words of any of the humans talking. I heard my Father from deep within me. I don't mean I always heard actual words—more like resonating impressions of love and joy. Sometimes there was the awareness of a need to correct a behavior or even to correct a thought. These impressions were never ever sharp, angry, or displeased reprimands. The only way I can think to describe the impressions I felt is to say that coupled with the enormous awareness of love for me came an awareness of areas in my life that were wrong for me because they hurt me. The anger or jealousy or bitterness I felt for others was most destructive to me! He didn't want me to hurt so I was encouraged to release all of those emotions to experience more joy and more completeness with HIM!

This revelation should have come as no surprise to me, really. The scriptures in the Bible teach that God has a *tremendous* love for us, as part of His creation. In the book of 1st John chapter 4, verse 8 we simply read, **"God is Love."** That's it. He is the source of love— the fulfillment of love. Love doesn't want the ones He loves to inflict pain on themselves. Bitterness brings pain. Jealousy and anger bring pain. I didn't need convincing. I was experiencing it. My pain within was a direct result of my own emotions toward others. Doesn't seem fair, does it? Others hurt us, we get angry and want to hurt back. But that very desire, that very first thought of anger, bitterness, and retaliation always made ME miserable. My thoughts were hurting me. So, as the impressions gently resonated around me, I was able to sense a delightful, joyous offer to love instead of being bitter. That offer of love—coupled with joy that I could feel—encouraged a letting go of the bitterness. I couldn't hold onto both emotions at the same time. That "letting go" was forgiveness.

If you're at all acquainted with the story of Jesus, you're aware that He claimed to be the Son of God. In fact, He claimed to BE one with God!! HALLELUJAH!! That assertion of deity, though, is what got him killed. The religious leaders of the day thought they were honoring God by killing Jesus. They thought He was very wrong and even evil to exalt Himself to the level of God. Jesus was killed by being nailed to two beams of wood that had been put together to form a cross. As he hung upon the cross, dying, Jesus prayed to God, His Father, to forgive those who had been responsible for putting Him on that cross. Forgiveness. Jesus made it clear. God never asks us to do anything He, Himself, isn't willing to do as well. Jesus knows exactly what it's like to forgive those who have wounded us. It's what He did. Jesus chose to love those who tortured and nailed Him to the cross to die.

As a young woman growing up, I had often heard the story of the crucifixion. So, when I felt wounded or wronged by someone, I usually sensed that internal, spiritual "nudge" to love and forgive as well. After all, that's what Jesus had done. I had come to realize that I am also a sinner needing forgiveness, and Jesus had died to take the punishment for me, too. Recalling the example of Jesus, I was able to grasp and, often, apply the suggestion.

The idea of the spiritual "nudge" causes some to wince. A nudge is personal. A nudge involves contact of some sort. Once again, I'm not saying I felt a physical touch or heard a voice. It all happened inside my head. It was thought contact. I believe I was experiencing thought contact with the Holy Spirit. Jesus Himself explained the actual indwelling of the Presence of the Spirit of God, the Holy Spirit, in John 14:16–17 when He explained that He (Jesus) would ask God to send His disciples a helper or an "Advocate," Who is the Spirit of Truth. This Spirit of Truth is also referred to a bit further down (verse 26) as the Holy Spirit. It is this Spirit of Truth/Holy Spirit Who will live *with* the disciples of Jesus and *in* us as well!!

> **And I will ask the Father, and he will give you another Advocate, who will never leave you. He is the Holy Spirit, who leads into all truth. The world cannot receive him, because it isn't looking for him and doesn't recognize him. But you know him, because he lives with you now and later will be in you** (John 14:16–17).

Jesus was getting ready to return to Heaven and promised His followers He would NOT leave them comfortless, as orphans, without someone to care for them. He would give them, or have sent to them, the very Spirit of God, Himself. The disciples of Jesus would *house* the communicative Presence of God *inside of them*!!

My awareness of the nature and character of God came both from His Spirit speaking/interacting with my spirit, inside of me, and from the words of the Bible itself. The Bible says that the scriptures are ALIVE! In the New Living Translation, the translation I use throughout the book in the 2015 edition unless otherwise indicated, we read:

> *For the word of God is alive and powerful. It is sharper than the sharpest two-edged sword, cutting between soul and spirit, between joint and marrow. It exposes our innermost thoughts and desires. Nothing in all creation is hidden from God. Everything is naked and exposed before his eyes, and he is the one to whom we are accountable. So then, since we have a great High Priest who has entered heaven, Jesus the Son of God, let us hold firmly to what we believe. This High Priest of ours understands our weaknesses, for he faced all of the same testings we do, yet he did not sin. So let us come boldly to*

the throne of our gracious God. There we will receive his mercy, and we will find grace to help us when we need it most (Hebrews 4:12–16).

Jesus says He is **the Way, the Truth, and the Life** (John 14:6). You cannot read the Bible, ask for oneness with Jesus, and not be confronted with a gradual awareness that you are in a living, intimate relationship with *another* spiritual being. That is, in addition to your own personal spirit living within your physical body, you become aware of another Presence within, without, and all around, assisting you. This Presence, the Holy Spirit, assists in the direction or **Way** you should take, tells you the **Truth** about the relationships and activities in your life, and helps you know how to deal with the moment-by-moment decisions of both minutia and substance that ultimately make up your **Life.**

You can't touch "It" or see "It", but you have an awareness of "It"—the Presence—or, to be correct, Him. Jesus explained before He left Earth that He

11

needed to leave in physical form so that the spiritual entity and Presence of the Holy Spirit could then come to Earth—they could not both inhabit earth simultaneously.

> *"But in fact, it is best for you that I go away, because if I don't, the Advocate won't come. If I do go away, then I will send him to you. And when he comes, he will convict the world of its sin, and of God's righteousness, and of the coming judgment. The world's sin is that it refuses to believe in me"* (John 16:7–9).

Jesus explained that the Holy Spirit would not be speaking on His own authority, but would share "what he has heard."

> *"When the Spirit of truth comes, he will guide you into all truth. He will not speak on his own but will tell you what he has heard. He will tell you about the future"* (John 16:13).

This verse shows us that what the Holy Spirit hears is from God the Father and from Jesus. THEY ARE ALL CONNECTED. More correctly, they are ONE.

Once again, prior to Jesus dying on that cross, He prepared His followers for what was about to happen. How kind! Don't you appreciate when you're told BEFORE something serious happens exactly WHAT is going to happen so you can be prepared?

I remember being in the hospital operating room as an adult, getting ready to undergo surgery. The anesthesiologist had just given me something to put me to sleep, and she began to talk to me. She told me my eyelids were going to get very heavy and it was ok to close them. They did and I did. Then she said I'd taste garlic in the back of my throat. Yep! Right again! I'm sure I'd awakened before this next series of thoughts came to me, but I began to wonder what would have happened if I'd had some dreaded association with garlic. There I was, about to undergo an operation, being put to sleep, virtually defenseless. What if she hadn't told me what to expect and in my altered state I had tasted the dreaded garlic. Would I have panicked? Possibly. Would I have associated garlic with death? Insanity? Maybe. Would I have fought the anesthesia? Would I have attempted to bolt from the bed? Who knows?? It's all possible. BUT the good news is that she HAD prepared me for the garlic. So, all was well.

Preparing His people ahead of time is what God did regularly throughout the Bible. He had Noah prepare for the flood. He had the Israelites prepare to leave Egypt after they'd been slaves there for 400 years. After three years of ministry, Jesus knew what was coming. After all, He's God! One of the most touching characteristics of Jesus was/is His humility. Even though Jesus had tremendous power, as evidenced by the many healings He performed, He routinely PRAYED or petitioned or made requests—talking about the concerns of His heart—to God, the Father.

It should come as no surprise, then, that, as Jesus got closer to His final moments on Earth, it was His

Father Who He approached and petitioned to carry out His wishes for the care of His followers after His death. He refers to them as His disciples. That means students. For a record of that complete conversation, I strongly encourage you to read all of John chapter 17. For now, I'll simply share a few verses:

> *"I am praying not only for these disciples but also for <u>all who will ever believe in me through their message</u>. I pray that they will all be one, just as you and I are one—as you are in me, Father, and I am in you. And may they be in us so that the world will believe you sent me. I have given them the glory you gave me, so they may be one as we are one. I am in them and you are in me. May they experience such perfect unity that the world will know that you sent me and that you love them as much as you love me"* (John 17:20–23, underlined by the author for emphasis).

Wonder of wonder!!! Jesus prayed for ME!! I'm someone who has come to believe in Jesus because of the testimony passed down from those original followers of Jesus!! HALLELUJAH!! Thank you Jesus!! Thank you for praying for me!!

And thank you, early followers, disciples, for SHARING THE GOOD NEWS of JESUS!! But wait. What Jesus prayed was for us to realize our ONENESS with Him—with Jesus—and with God the Father! Jesus prayed for all His followers to be IN HIM as He, Jesus, is IN GOD and God is IN Jesus.

What does it mean to be IN? According to the Cambridge English Dictionary, to be "in" is to be "inside a container, place, or area, or surrounded or closed off by something."[1] In this case, to be IN, is to be INSIDE the MIND, the THINKING of JESUS— THE THINKING OF GOD!!

Wait! God is omnipotent—ALL powerful! He's omniscient—ALL knowing. HOW is it possible for any of us to be situated within the inner thoughts of God? I'm not suggesting for us to be in God is to know everything God knows or thinks. Let's listen to the Apostle Paul as he explains:

But it was to us that God revealed these things by his Spirit. For his Spirit searches out everything and shows us God's deep secrets. No one can know a person's thoughts except that person's own spirit, and no one can know God's thoughts except God's own Spirit. And we have received God's Spirit (not the world's spirit), so we can know the wonderful things God has freely given us.

When we tell you these things, we do not use words that come from human wisdom. Instead, we speak words given to us by the Spirit, using the Spirit's words to explain spiritual truths. But people who aren't spiritual can't receive these truths from God's Spirit. It all sounds foolish to them and they can't understand it, for only those who are spiritual can understand what the Spirit means. Those who are spiritual can evaluate all things, but they themselves cannot be evaluated by others. For,

"Who can know the LORD'S thoughts?
Who knows enough to teach him?"

But we understand these things, for we have the mind of Christ (1 Corinthians 2:10–16).

The MIND of Christ!! We're able to receive the very thoughts of Jesus! Amazing!!

So, not only are the scriptures alive as we recently saw looking at Hebrews 4:12 but also the Holy Spirit—who was promised to us by Jesus in John 16:13—actually enters into us, takes up residence, and begins communicating with/to/for our own personal spirit in language the Apostle Paul describes in Romans as "too deep for words."

> *And the Holy Spirit helps us in our weakness. For example, we don't know what God wants us to pray for. But the Holy Spirit prays for us with groanings that cannot be expressed in words. And the Father who knows all hearts knows what the Spirit is saying, for the Spirit pleads for us believers in harmony with God's own will* (Romans 8:26–27).

The Holy Spirit searches our hearts, and recognizes our thoughts, feelings, fears, hopes, dreams, favorite colors, scents, touches—everything. He then communicates all of that to God the Father. He—the

Holy Spirit—is our connection to the Creator of the universe. The Spirit of God is active and alive and interacts with our spirit. The communication happens in the inner man, also known as the mind, soul, or spirit. The Spirit of God is active in both the written, living words of the Bible and in the living Spirit of God, Who indwells each individual who loves and obeys God.

"...The Holy Spirit, who is given by God to those who obey Him" (Acts 5:32).

Even when I was young, I read my Bible and found myself particularly drawn to explanations of the activity of the Holy Spirit. I know now that He is God Within!! I read with total joy at how He gave direction to the early Christians as to where to go and what to do. In Acts 8:29, we read of the Holy Spirit telling the Apostle Phillip which chariot to approach. In Acts 11:28, we're told that a prophet named Agabus predicted—by the Spirit—that a great famine was coming upon the entire Roman world. In Acts 13:2–4, we learn that as a gathering of Christians were praying, they were told by the Holy Spirit to send two men named Barnabas and Saul on a special assignment by Him. In the book of Acts, we read of that kind of thing happening over and over again.

I wanted Him to give ME direction. I loved my sense of His Presence with me, but I wanted more. I wanted more than just impressions of His love for me and His desire for me to love those around me. I wanted Him to give me ideas as to HOW to love. I wanted more of Him in everything.

I prayed for direction. I yearned for direction. I wondered: *Would I marry? Who was I to marry? When? Where was I to live? What was to be my life's work? Should I be a missionary? What was I to DO?*

One night I had a dream. In the dream I cried out and cried out and cried out to God for direction. Silence. No answer. No impression. Nothing. Disappointed and disgusted, I turned to walk away. I was so disappointed with Him. He *knew* I needed Him.

He *knew* I honestly *wanted* to hear from Him *and* He knew I was willing to obey! How could He, knowing of my love for Him, and knowing my need for Him, *not* give me *something*?? He was rude! I remember thinking, *Well, I've always depended on God, but He doesn't want to have anything to do with me, so from now on I'm not having anything to do with* **Him**! In the instant that I was thinking those thoughts and turning to walk away—with absolutely **no** idea as to whom or what I would now look to for guidance—a brilliant shaft of light pierced the darkness from Heaven to the exact spot from which I had just lifted my foot. In fact, I had only stepped with my right foot, pivoted on the toe of my left foot and begun to lift that heel when the light shot forth.

It was Him!! I was overjoyed! I felt connected! Comforted! He *had* heard me, and He *was* responding to *me*!! I reached out to touch the light, and it had substance!! (This experience was actually the inspiration for the cover that a friend of mine painted.) As soon as my hand touched the light, it lifted me up and carried me high above the world. I looked down and saw a very dark universe and a dark planet with pin points of brilliant light sparkling intermittently around the planet. The instruction that came to me was still not an audible voice, but more like a thought that simply told me to tell people on Earth about the good God Whom I love and love to serve.

When the shaft of light first appeared, I remember wondering if I had been covering up the light with my heel. Had the light needed me to move for it to shine forth? OR was it that God, up in Heaven, had determined to touch the Earth on the exact spot on which I had been standing, but He required my movement before He would/could send the light? In either case, my movement had been necessary.

That lone thought about the necessity of my movement has been helpful to me through the years. Whenever I have pondered and pondered what to do, it has occurred to me that I must do *something* and, if that action is wrong, then I can expect God to stop me and turn me around to "see the light," but if the action is right, I can expect Him to bless and encourage me. Pondering and sitting and doing nothing except waiting for guidance has not been the way God best interacts with me. In my case, God has affirmed, time and time again, that He IS listening and He *is* acting. If I'll just step out—maybe not even knowing where or how to go, but staying connected to Him in my thoughts, He *will* communicate to me and show me what He wants.

Following God's Plan for Us

I pray that writing this book is a part of me holding onto that shaft of light (that I saw in my dream) and traveling around the world to tell people about God. I had prayed repeatedly for God to tell me what to do. I desperately wanted to know His plan for my life. I'm an old woman now. I've been thinking about writing this book for a very long time. If what I'm writing is pleasing to God, then He will bless the words I put together, regardless of how long it has taken me to get to this point. He's a good Father. He's patient.

Perhaps you, too, have been calling out to our Father asking Him for direction for your life. We are never too old to listen, to humble ourselves and receive direction from Him! Noah, Abraham, and Moses were all old men when the Lord gave them their missions! If you're just starting out, or have been walking down life's road for a while, God has a plan for you!

> *"For I know the plans I have for you," says the LORD. "They are plans for good and not for disaster, to give you a future and a hope"* (Jeremiah 29:11).

John the Baptist had been conceived and brought into this world for one purpose and one mission only: to prepare the way for the Lord—to be the forerunner of Jesus (Luke 1:13–17). He lived in the desert and he preached nonstop for the people to get ready because someone wonderful was coming—soon (Luke 3:3–18).

John actually baptized Jesus. They knew each other. They were cousins (Luke 1:26–44).

John was not a man to mince words. After baptizing Jesus, he was arrested because he spoke out against the lifestyle of the political leader of the community: King Herod. Herod had married his brother Phillip's wife and John had the audacity to tell him/them they were living in sin! When John was in prison, he continued to think about his main mission: preparing the people for the coming of the Messiah. He had referred to Jesus as the one who came to take away the sins of the world.

> *The next day John saw Jesus coming toward him and said, "Look! The Lamb of God who takes away the sin of the world!"* (John 1:29).

BUT, now that he was in prison, with darkness all around, some element of doubt seemed to begin to needle John. He must have pondered about what to think and what to do. Finally, John sent friends to Jesus to ask Him, straight out, if He, in fact, was the Messiah—the Son of God.

Jesus didn't reprimand either John or his friends for asking this question. Instead, He simply told them to look around and see what was happening:

> **Then he told John's disciples, "Go back to John and tell him what you have seen and heard—the blind see,** (light!) **the lame walk, those with leprosy are cured, the deaf hear, the dead are raised to life, and the Good News is being preached to the poor."** (Luke 7:22, parenthetical word added by the author).

Jesus was pointing out that an enormous amount of power was coming out of Him to do good—lots and lots of good!! John knew the scriptures as well as anyone. John knew that prophets who had lived hundreds of years earlier had predicted that the Messiah would come doing miraculous wonders (Isaiah 45:4, 5, 6). Jesus was fulfilling prophesy. Jesus was, in fact, the long awaited Messiah. To comfort and convince John, Jesus simply told John's friends to tell John what they were seeing and hearing. So simple. So practical. Just tell or communicate what is happening around you.

Miracles. Power. Communication with and about God. All were so basic to Jesus' ministry and so imperative to convincing people that He was who He said He was. Yet, how much time do portions of the organized church spend in either encouraging or teaching such communication? How often are we, the followers of Jesus, told about miracles or power or answers to prayer or simply internal communication with our Father? We are taught to lean on Him, learn of Him through His Word, trust Him, obey Him, love Him, honor, adore, and worship Him. We're taught to pray to Him, even fear Him. But encouragement to talk to God and LISTEN to Him for a reply is actually feared in, of all places, the church. The church should be the safest place to share our walk with God. Instead, much of the time, people in the church are afraid of being labeled "kook" if they speak out in such terminology as "I believe God put (such and such) on my heart" or "God showed His power in my life by…"

etc. Some think such comments open the door for abuses.

Abuses

Some ask, "What about those who clearly did *not* hear from God to do or say such and such but say that they *have* heard from God?" The Bible teaches us about God. The Bible teaches us about the Holy Spirit as well. Furthermore, we *experience* the indwelling of the Holy Spirit. Although we may have experienced the Holy Spirit, much that we've learned about Him is from the Bible. The Holy Spirit will never do or share anything that is contrary to the scriptures. Jesus refers to the Holy Spirit as the Spirit of Truth (John 14:17). He also refers to the Word of God as being "Truth." Therefore, if the scriptures (the written Word of God), are truth, and the Spirit of God is also truth—they *cannot* contradict each other!

Furthermore, the scriptures themselves give guidelines as to how to know whether or not someone is speaking information communicated by the Holy Spirit. These guidelines say to confirm the information by the impressions of several prophets:

> ***Let two or three people prophesy, and let the others evaluate what is said*** (1 Corinthians 14:29).

Still, some church leaders seem to fear that false sharing might take place. Therefore, they stifle all of it.

Then there is that group within Christendom that simply says "nope, that doesn't happen anymore. The Holy Spirit *once* talked to Christians back when the early church was being started, but He doesn't do that anymore. Furthermore, miracles don't occur anymore, either." The problem with that perspective is that there are those of us who *have* experienced His miraculous intervention, *have* heard from Him, and *do* communicate with Him on an ongoing basis—we *know* He's still active. That's like telling a married woman that her husband doesn't exist because the neighbors have never seen him. She sees him, touches him, cares for him is cared for by him, has evidence all around her that he exists, and someone dares to tell her he's someone she made up. Those of us in the church who have experienced communication/contact with God, who then hear that the Holy Spirit HAD activity that He reserved ONLY for the early church but that He doesn't share with us today, merely sit and sigh in sadness.

That idea or habit of saying, "No, He doesn't interact with us personally anymore," is worse than simply causing some of us to be sad. It is, I believe, full-out wrong. If we say something doesn't happen or hasn't happened, which others say HAS happened, then we're calling those people liars who claim to have had those experiences. That's wrong. Likewise, if we say something happened that didn't happen, that's wrong, too. In the book of 1 Thessalonians, the Apostle Paul writes:

Do not stifle the Holy Spirit (1 Thessalonians 5:19).

Merriam-Webster defines stifle as "to withhold from circulation or expression."[2] Other Bible translations use the word, "quench." As in:

Do not quench the Holy Spirit (1 Thessalonians 5:19, NASB).

To quench, according to Merriam-Webster, "is to put out or extinguish."[3] Saying "NO! NO! NO!" to the Holy Spirit repeatedly is to stifle Him or, even extinguish Him in a person's life.

In the corridors of the church buildings, in our homes, and in private fellowships, those of us who have experienced the activity of the Holy Spirit seek out others who believe and have experienced as we do and have. We share the impressions we've had and the thoughts that have come to us from _Him_. After we share, we smile and we feel blessed, but we want _more_.

We want open fellowship and open sharing. We believe it is God, Himself, who is whispering to us, "there is more," and we yearn to participate in that more.

Still, there are those who refuse to believe it possible that God would/could/should communicate to us in our brains. They say things like: "Why does God speak to you, Mary, and not to me? How come I can't hear Him? Why doesn't He speak in an audible voice so we can *all* hear Him?" Mostly, I don't know. *But*, I'm wondering if it's possible that God *is* speaking to the majority of Christians and they just haven't learned to recognize His voice. I wonder if the scenario would be similar to a person whose first language is not English, who didn't know "wind" by that name, and was asked: "Do you have a lot of wind in this area?" He may respond: "No, we don't have any," simply because he didn't really understand what was being asked him.

As I have shared these concerns with a dear friend of mine, she began to wonder if what she has been calling "conscience" all these years was really the Holy

Spirit speaking to her heart. One day, another friend of mine offered to take my (then) little girl to an ice cream parlor. When she said the name of the ice cream place, I told her I had no idea where it was. She looked at me in disbelief and said, "But Mary! *You're* the one who showed it to *me!*" Then, when she went on to explain the location of the ice cream shop, I understood exactly what she meant. The problem? I had known the ice cream parlor by a previous name. The new name threw me. Once she explained where it was located, and the quality of the ice cream, I knew *exactly* what she was talking about.

I'm wondering if Christians aren't struggling with the same misunderstandings. The problem, of course, is that if we're convinced that the inner pangs we sometimes feel for behaving in a particular way simply originate from our own "conscience," then we may be under the mistaken notion that God isn't involved. We do know that not every thought comes from God. However, there *is* a way to know which thoughts are from Him! How well I recall a time when I was extremely frustrated with my husband. I began rehearsing in my head how I was going to present my argument for whatever it was he had done, and how he was going to be forced to look at the truth of the matter.

Just as I thought my argument was set, I sensed a question from the Lord. It seemed to me that He was asking me if He, Jesus, would be honored in what I was about to do/say. I nearly rolled my eyes. OF COURSE He would be honored! I was going to be speaking TRUTH to David! Jesus IS Truth! Jesus would DEFINITELY be on "my side." I was armed with truth and I was ready to wield it as a club! At that point, I sensed a whispered question: *Was the plan truly from God?*

A bell started going off in my head. Something from the Bible…something about wisdom from above. I looked it up and began to choke on my war whoop.

> *But the wisdom from above is first of all pure. It is also peace loving, gentle at all times, and willing to yield to others. It is full of mercy and the fruit of good deeds. It shows no favoritism and is always sincere* (James 3:17).

Busted. That description of wisdom from above did *not* reflect the thoughts in my brain. I knew I was *not* in harmony with the Holy Spirit and that I needed to ask Him for help. There wasn't one thing peaceable or gentle about my plan of attack. And a planned attack is exactly what it was. I sighed and rethought how I should go about sharing my hurt and concern with David. I've even forgotten what the issue or problem was. I only know it didn't turn into an ugly confrontation between us because my Lord encouraged me to truly think about my heart, my words, and my actions.

If anyone wonders about the purity of his/her thoughts, we have only to look to the scriptures in the Bible for guidance once again.

The words of the LORD are pure (Psalms 12:6, NASB).

The commandment of the LORD is pure, enlightening the eyes (Psalm 19:8, NASB).

Are we aligned with the Word of God?

Do the majority of our thoughts agree or align themselves with the Word of God—the BIBLE? OR do our thoughts align themselves with the teachings of the people around us? If we're mostly thinking thoughts promoted by those around us or our culture at large, we will, eventually, find ourselves without any foundation for the direction of our thinking or our lives. We'll be blown about by the whims of society.

I am convinced James 3:17, that I quoted in the last section, saved my marriage. Often. I'm also certain that the Lord used that particular scripture to save other family relationships as well. I recall a time when I was particularly frustrated with one of my daughters. She was a fully-grown, married woman with children, and she had either done something or hadn't done something that I found very troubling. I remember calling out to the Lord to help me. He reminded me of James 3:17, so I knew I must not lash out at her in anger. I also knew I did NOT want to allow the matter to simply blow over. I needed to "confront" her with the matter. But how? Every single comment I pondered internally sounded harsh and condemning. I decided to say nothing until the Lord, Himself, "gave me" the right words to say.

As I recall, I prayed for three days, asking Him repeatedly to please tell me how to proceed. I finally said, out loud, "Lord, please help me here, cause on my own, I got nothin'!" Finally, on the third day of my petition, a question popped into my head. It was a simple, non-threatening question that I believe He was encouraging me to ask my daughter. As I recall, it was something like, "Would you mind, please, to explain your thinking to me as to why you…" (whatever it was). "I really want to understand." I think I went into additional detail as to why the matter had puzzled me in the first place.

I still recall my daughter's look of shock as she calmly listened to my question. But, best of all, I remember her response. She immediately, with kindness, said, "Oh! I'm sorry!" and went on to explain her take on the matter. My insides had been tangled up for three days, but my Lord intervened and whispered a question for me to share with my daughter that gently unraveled the tangle. The possibility for a family blow-up had definitely been calling out to me, but, thankfully, my Lord came to my aid and showed me a better way. This scripture is so important, it bears repeating. Here it is in another version.

> **Wisdom that comes from heaven is first of all pure…gentle…**(James 3:17, NASB).

My Lord had first of all pointed me to the scriptures, the Bible, for my heart direction on the matter. THEN, however, upon hearing my plea for further direction,

He spoke to my heart in a way that I could hear and understand so that I could ask my daughter for clarification. She then apologized and explained what her understanding had been of the matter. No harm, no foul. Jesus met me inside my own head and led me away from a potential verbal attack on my daughter!

If we want God to help direct our thinking, we're going to need to hold up our thoughts to see if they align with the Word of God. And we're going to need to humbly ask God for guidance.

Repeat the following full verse:

> *Wisdom that comes from heaven is first of all pure, then peace loving, gentle at all times, willing to yield to others. It is full of mercy and good deeds. It shows no partiality and is always sincere* (James 3:17, NASB).

Let's hold up the Bible, a lamp to our feet and a light for our paths, as we are instructed to do (Psalm

119:105). As we do, we will learn the truth about our thoughts, as the book of Hebrews says:

> *For the word of God is alive and powerful. It is sharper than the sharpest two-edged sword, cutting between soul and spirit, between joint and marrow. It exposes our innermost thoughts and desires* (Hebrews 4:12).

If we ever think we may be having a communication from God, first and foremost, we must go to the written Word, the Bible. We will need to look at passages that have to do with the matter at hand to learn if that communication lines up with what has been passed down to us by His Holy Spirit throughout the ages. It is no wonder that the former shepherd and later King of Israel, David, referred to God as his Rock, his Salvation, his Fortress where he, (David) would never be shaken (Psalm 62:2). God's Word is firm. It is sure. It is steady. We can go back to it over and over again.

Just as David was looking for a refuge in God, if you are a loving, concerned parent, you want more than anything to keep your child safe, well cared for, and aware of your love for him/her. If you knew that you would be away from the child for a while, you would arrange the best of care for the child in your absence. While you were away you would call or e-mail, do FaceTime, or engage in some means of technological visual communication. You might even send snail mail. Suppose you were to go somewhere that didn't have telephone or electronic access, *and* suppose that the mail was unreliable. How would you communicate with your child? You would likely send a messenger— someone you trusted to convey your love to your child. But, what if your messenger got sick or quit?

Now think of Jehovah God of the universe and His unlimited resources. He created a being He loved more than all His other creations. He made the being— man—in such a way, however, that man cannot make the decisions he needs to learn to make if he can see God. So, God made a decision to make Himself virtually invisible to mankind. BUT we're His creation and He loves us. God wants to protect us, guide us, and communicate His love for us *to* us. How would He do that? He could semi-appear and actually speak to a select few and ask them to tell the others. He could send messengers—and He did.

Starting in the book of Genesis and going through Revelation, the Bible tells us of communications God had with mankind through various means. Adam, Eve, Noah and Abraham saw Him face to face. Moses saw Him through a burning bush and later in bodily form. Gideon saw an angel, Deborah received specific information as to how to conduct battles. Samuel heard a whisper, and Isaiah saw visions of angels and the Lord. Jeremiah experienced visions and heard the spoken Word. Daniel had visions, saw an angel, and received the spoken Word. Ezekiel, Jesus, Paul, John, Peter, and others also experienced communication from God in myriad ways. God gave these men and women messages that He wanted them to share with those around them—and they did! The point is that

God found various means to communicate to His children to let them know that He was watching them. He was aware of what they were going through and what they needed. He then communicated how He would provide for them. He loved them.

In addition to messengers, God also *has* unlimited resources at His disposal. Why not fashion the people he created to have brains that operate in such a way that they can actually receive transmissions directly from their Creator: the GOD of the UNIVERSE? They would have no need for phones or e-mail. We're talking *thought* mail! From God's brain/heart to His creation's in less than a heartbeat. Recall, once again, in one of the Apostle Paul's letters, where we read:

> *But it was to us that God revealed these things by his Spirit. For his Spirit searches out everything and shows us God's deep secrets. No one can know a person's thoughts except that person's own spirit, and no one can know God's thoughts except God's own Spirit. And we have received God's Spirit (not the world's spirit), so we*

can know the wonderful things God has freely given us. When we tell you these things, we do not use words that come from human wisdom. Instead, we speak words given to us by the Spirit, using the Spirit's words to explain spiritual truths (1 Corinthians 2:10–13).

"Words given to us by the Spirit." How? Are they spoken out loud? Do these words arrive via messenger or through a church sanctioned publication? Or, do these words just come into the brain? It seems that the experience is just that—a thought, an awareness, or a direction that hadn't been there earlier. Note too that Paul, in the verses we just read in 1 Corinthians, describes the activity of the Holy Spirit in *the present,* not the past tense: "… His Spirit *searches* out everything and *shows* us even God's deep secrets…" Spiritual truths from *The Spirit.* Now *that's* communication!! *That's* CURRENT contact!!

Does communication from God still take place? There are many groups of people and churches that have always maintained that it does. However, some churches espouse cessationism, which means that God has ceased or stopped communicating **directly** to mankind. Those churches mostly teach about the "indwelling" presence of the Holy Spirit without ever encouraging their church members to consider what all that might entail. (See the last passage referenced, 1 Corinthians 2:10-13, about the Holy Spirit living within people or indwelling their/our bodies to reveal spiritual understanding to us.) However, such limited teaching was only from men. God, Himself, has been at work within His people assuring us of His love for us, and His desire to lead and enlighten us. *And He has* enlightened us.

The problem, I think, is that we aren't *telling others* about our contact or guidance from Him. Why not? At the time I wrote the bulk of this book, the answer, I believe, from my own particular church group, to the question, "Why wouldn't I tell anyone?", is that—for the most part—no one was asking. Within that body of believers, I have no memory of ever sitting in a Bible class where the teacher asked "How has God communicated His love to you this week?" Or "Do any of you believe God has communicated something to you which He intends for you to share with the rest of us?" In fact, I suspect that even to ask such a question would be perceived, by some, as "getting away from the scriptures." How sad. Jesus said it best:

> *"You search the Scriptures because you think they give you eternal life. But the Scriptures point to me!"* (John 5:39).

The scriptures themselves point to Jesus as being the Son of God. Jesus actually claimed to be *"THE WAY, THE TRUTH and THE LIFE"* (John 14:6, capitalized by the author for emphasis). Jesus pointed to the Holy Spirit as being the indwelling communicator of Truth. Jesus also said:

> *"the Truth will set you free!"* (John 8:32).

How many of us would *love* to be free from something—worry, illness, loneliness, or stress—but we fail to tap into the *One* power that has been appointed to free us! Furthermore, when we *do* tap into the power, we often fail to tell others about it, therefore denying Jesus the opportunity to receive praise and credit for our deliverance! In addition, sometimes we fail to pass along the spiritual tool to our brothers and sisters. In these situations, we could do better to equip each other if we consider the following questions: Have we prayed? Is there a particular scripture that is enlightening and providing direction? Have we simply sought solitude and been alone with God for a day or two? Have we been prayed over by someone who seemed to have a gift for healing? Have we been freed from some type of demonic harassment?

Are We Telling the Goodness of God to Others?

When John's disciples came to Jesus asking for confirmation as to whether or not He was the Messiah,

Jesus said, in effect "Look at the power." Jesus promised the indwelling of the Holy Spirit to His followers. Power accompanies the Holy Spirit. Luke 4:14 talks about Jesus being filled with the Holy Spirit's power. In Acts 1:8, Jesus tells the apostles they will receive power when the Holy Spirit has come upon them. In John 14:12, it is recorded that Jesus promised that *anyone* who believes in Him will do the same works He did—and even *greater works*. He also encouraged His followers to ask *anything* in His name and He would do it!! Now *that's* power!!

However, scriptures also teach that a time would come when some people would act as if they are religious, but would reject the power that could make them godly.

In the last days there will be very difficult times. For people will love only themselves and their money. They will be boastful and proud, scoffing at God, disobedient to their parents, and ungrateful. They will consider nothing sacred. They will be unloving and unforgiving; they will slander others and have no self-control. They will be cruel and hate what is good. They will betray their friends, be reckless, be puffed up with pride, and love pleasure rather than God. They will act religious, but they will reject the power that could make them godly. Stay away from people like that (2 Timothy 3:1–5).

Reject the power. Reject the Holy Spirit. Reject the indwelling comfort of the Eternal Savior. Reject the wellness. Reject the wholeness. Reject the internal whispering of the great I Am. All of this rejection doesn't mean He has stopped whispering. It may simply mean that we aren't listening.

Chapter Two

COMMUNICATION FROM GOD– WHAT FORM DOES IT TAKE?

Question: When God decides to communicate with His children, what form does that communication take?

Answer: Any form He chooses!

When God wanted to talk to Moses, he got his attention by igniting a bush, but not burning it up. Once Moses approached the bush, the voice that came out of it was a REAL attention-getter!

What's the logical inference if this story were all we knew about God? When God wants to talk to mankind, He sets a bush on fire and then talks out of it. That's not exactly the case, but stick with me here.

There was also the time that God wanted to let the Israelites know they could fully depend on Him to deliver them—forever—from being enslaved by the Egyptians. He parted the Red Sea and let them cross over—and out of Egypt—on dry ground.

What's the logical deduction from this story? When God wants to show His power, He will lead mankind to a body of water and then part it for them.

Umm, well, there was also the time David had sinned by committing adultery with Bathsheba and God sent Nathan, the prophet, to confront David with his sin. He didn't use a bush or a sea—just another human being.

Then too, there was the time God wanted to tell Mary that she would be the mother of His son. He sent her an angel to explain everything.

And how about when Jesus was baptized? God sent His Spirit in the form of a dove to rest on Jesus, and then God spoke—some said it thundered—and God simply announced that Jesus was His beloved son.

Now what's the logical deduction? God is creative! He is not limited to a particular way of communicating or revealing Himself to mankind.

At various times in my life, and I KNOW I am not alone here, I have had secret thoughts—maybe a wish or a question about something—a thought that I never told anyone. Then, one day, out of the blue, that thought was answered or the desired something was presented to me—within attainable reach. I have often smiled at God and thanked Him for His graciousness to me. Let me share two stories that illustrate how God unexpectedly answered my thoughts.

The summer before I started the ninth grade, our house was hit by lightning one morning, and the upper level of our home was badly burned. Between fire damage and water damage from the water required to put out the fire, our house went from being "home" to being condemned as unsuitable for human occupancy. Yet, before nightfall, our friends and neighbors helped us locate and move into a comfortable house located within the "heart" of our small town's downtown area. I remember checking out that house and discovering, to my total surprise, well-placed boards were nailed to a tree just outside the bedroom window where I was to stay. The boards made perfect "steps" from the window to just a few feet from the ground! "HOW COOL!" I'd always dreamed of having my own room with some kind of a secret room attached, or tunnel to somewhere fabulous, or tree, or SOMETHING special. I'd never told anyone, but GOD knew!! AND as an extreme bonus, with our insurance to take care of all the damage, my mom and dad were able to make improvements on our burned house that maybe they'd thought about, but I had never heard them utter. Anyway, MANY blessings came from that lightning strike. Blessings we'd never talked about...only thought about.

As I wrote this story about our house when I was growing up, I felt a little nudge by the Lord. He was reminding me of another story...my most unexpected blessing—my husband, David! It's true! The truth is that I had been VERY specific about what I was looking for in a husband. I had talked to God often about my "list." It was a real list, too! Formidable, even! In fact, I'd looked at it, sighed and concluded, "You don't make them like that anymore, do you, God?" Had I been Catholic, I'm sure I would have looked at that list and then gone off to join a nunnery. I was asking for the impossible. I wanted my someone to be a godly man but not haughty. Not full of himself or so sure of his understanding of scripture that he left no room for the activity of the Holy Spirit. I needed him to be bright. I'm a strong-willed woman, but if the man has a hefty amount of intellect, I've been known to yield to his opinion. I also wanted him to enjoy sports AND have a very good sense of humor. Moan. I didn't see anyone able to meet the challenge.

Enter David Tao. I was totally blind-sighted when he asked me out. I had never cast a flirtatious eye his direction. David received his undergrad degree at

Harvard. I know how to spell Harvard. That's my link to it. He also loved (and still loves) the Lord, is open to the movement of the Holy Spirit, loves basketball with a passion, and has an amazing wit. To top it off, he's basically a concert pianist. AND he's the son of two phenomenally generous people. David's parents made it possible for our entire family (David, me, and our four children) to visit England and China. On and on...I never saw any of that coming. I never even THOUGHT to ask about the travel or music ability.

BUT, there have been times—way more than there should have been—when I have doubted my decision to marry David. I have asked, *God, are You SURE it was YOUR will for me to marry him??* I was so concerned about God's approval of our marriage that I finally asked God to grant me a "sign." I told him I needed something from Him to ASSURE me that He, God, had chosen David for me. I thought of something that ONLY GOD could do. I asked to have a baby born on our wedding anniversary if, in fact, David was the man

I was to go through life with. Sure enough, our youngest child was born smack in the middle of an ice storm on January 13th, 1988—our 15th wedding anniversary.

Only He—the discerner of secret thoughts—and some not-so-secret—could have known what my deep down interests/concerns/worries were…AND He invariably presented me with not only what I THOUGHT I wanted/needed but also gave me more than I had initially imagined. How often this "more than enough" answer happened to members of the church I attended the majority of my life, I have no idea—because we had no forum for sharing such experiences with one another. The point, however, is that God DID respond to me, and He DID address my thoughts because He knew them! That is listening and responding activity—communication—from God!

Here's another interesting observation: When Jesus walked the Earth, He had a habit of being around needy people and ASKING them what they wanted! Matthew

20:32 tells of two blind men sitting by the side of the road, calling out to Jesus as He passed by. They were BLIND but Jesus asked them what they wanted. Jesus did the same thing with a blind fellow named Bartimaeus. He was also calling out to Jesus for help—that story is recorded in Mark 10:51. Jesus seems to want the needful men to hear themselves state their need. That way, when the need was met, they could be certain that Jesus had responded specifically to their own request. Jesus made it personal. Or, perhaps in initiating the verbalization of a request, He was allowing the individual to dare to hope for a change in his/her situation.

I'm not exactly sure how or when I began taking my little, seemingly inconsequential concerns to God. But once I started, I never stopped. I have a zillion memories of asking God to help me locate something I'd misplaced. I even have a favorite expression I use: "Lord, I've done it again. I don't know where I've put (fill in the blank), but I know YOU do! So, please, Lord, help me find it." AND the vast majority of the time, He does!!

One of my favorite "finds" was the time a bunch of us were playing volleyball on the grass at a park in St. Louis. My then boyfriend, David, suddenly called "TIME" and announced he'd just lost his contact lens. Everyone stopped immediately and began looking around to try and find it. Silently, I prayed, *Oh Lord, help ME be the one to find it!* (I needed that fellow to realize he needed me!!) After a couple of minutes David called off the search and encouraged us all to resume the game. Sighing, I stood up, looked down one last time, and there, exactly in front of the toe of my tennis shoe was that contact lens!!! THANK YOU, GOD!! Is it any wonder that after we'd married and had children, I found myself praying to find clean underwear for them on rushed school day mornings? Or that, on nearing suppertime I'd stare into the pantry and whisper, "Lord, YOU know what's in here! What in the world can I make with any of this?" Ideas would come! Blessings from Heaven—time after time after time.

The particular concerns I just shared may seem trivial and some may find my communication with my Father almost insulting. I've heard some people suggest that our Lord is too busy for the trivial concerns of our lives. Here's the problem with that: MY WHOLE LIFE IS DEALING WITH THE TRIVIAL!! If I don't learn to take the trivial to God, to Jesus and the Holy Spirit, I've shut Him out of the MAJORITY of my life!! No! He cares about ME! Jesus is recorded to have said (in Matthew 10:30) that even the hairs of our head are numbered!! GOD IS INTERESTED IN THE MINUTIA OF EACH OF US!

What Are You Asking God For?

Here are some questions for you:

What do you want Jesus to do for you?

Are you asking Him for help?

Are you prepared to receive His help?

As we ask ourselves these questions, let's look at a biblical example to help us consider our motives. In Chapter 8 of the book of Acts, we're told about Simon, who had witnessed the Holy Spirit being given to people upon whom the apostles had laid their hands. After these people received the Holy Spirit, Simon then offered the apostles money so that he would also have the ability to impart the Holy Spirit to others. Simon asked. Simon wanted. However, what Simon received was a stern rebuke: Peter told him "NO!" Why? Simon had asked for the Holy Spirit "so that everyone on whom I lay my hands may receive the Holy Spirit" (Acts 8:19, NASB). Prior to witnessing the apostles laying hands on the people, Simon had been convicted of his need for Jesus and had actually been baptized. He then followed one of the disciples, Philip, "everywhere" observing the good he did. As soon as he witnessed the Holy Spirit being received by those on whom the apostles laid their hands, he recognized this action as a good thing and wanted it himself. It sounds as if he was wanting to bless lives.

However, Peter rebuked Simon because he (Simon) thought the Holy Spirit could be bought and sold. He thought the Holy Spirit was controlled by Peter and John, and his perception was that they, in turn, could be persuaded (controlled) by money. Simon's actions revealed that although he'd been very impressed with the power of the Holy Spirit, he still thought that money was the greater power, because he thought it could buy and sell this power. Peter explained to Simon that his request revealed a bitter heart, which was still captive to sin. How could Peter conclude that Simon's heart was full of bitterness?

Here are a few thoughts: If one believes that money is the ultimate power, then having money should bring ultimate power. If ultimate power is seen as good, then having sufficient money to possess ultimate power would also be seen as good. However, if you do not have sufficient money to, somehow, obtain "ultimate power," (however you envision that) and others do, and ultimate power is what you want, wouldn't it be reasonable to believe that jealousy would be your constant companion? Isn't jealousy—desiring what others have, wishing they didn't have it and you did— a precursor of bitterness? James, the brother of Jesus, even couples bitterness with jealousy when he says:

> **If you are bitterly jealous and there is selfish ambition in your hearts...**(James 3:14).

Bitterness and jealousy seem to go together!

How did Peter figure all that out so quickly? I suggest it was the Holy Spirit within Peter, educating him, so that he knew how to respond to Simon.

Here are some questions to ask yourself: Do you need? Do you want? Are you asking? If you're not receiving, it may be time for a "heart check." What do your requests of God really reveal about your heart?

Let's take a moment to look at the heart of Philip. You may recall that before Simon had been chastised by Peter for the wickedness of his heart, Simon had been following Philip around, observing all the good he, Philip, was doing. Then, suddenly, Philip was given a new "order," in Acts 8:

> **As for Philip, an angel of the LORD said to him, "Go south down the desert road that runs from Jerusalem to Gaza"** (Acts 8:26).

A few verses later, it says:

> **The Holy Spirit said to Philip, "Go over and walk along beside the carriage"** (Acts 8:29).

In a single day, Philip received communication from both an angel and the Holy Spirit. In both instances, he was given fairly specific instructions about a desert road and a carriage. After listening to what was happening in THAT carriage, Philip began to speak to the individual and shared the good news of Jesus with the man. We aren't told that Philip had been asking for direction; we're simply told that he was given an assignment.

WHAT FORM DOES IT TAKE?

Earlier in the chapter, the text mentions Simon being among crowds of people who listened to Philip preach and observed him perform miracles. Suddenly, however, in verse 26, Philip is told to take off down a desert road—and he's not told why. When one is in the midst of popularity and crowd pleasing miracles, it hardly seems the time to retreat into the desert. Nonetheless, Philip quickly obeyed. He must have had a willing heart. He must have had an obedient heart. He certainly had a receptive heart to the instruction of the Holy Spirit. Philip obeyed and another soul was added to the Kingdom. God called Philip to leave the crowd and go teach the one. Leaving was illogical. The hordes were in the city. More people would be blessed if he had remained in the city. Nonetheless, for no apparent reason, an angel said "go" and Phillip went. The Holy Spirit said "go…and stay near…" and Phillip did.

Oh to have a willing heart like Philip! Philip looked and listened for the opportunity to be useful in the Kingdom and then he responded to it. He

RESPONDED to the opportunity. He didn't initiate it, he RESPONDED to it. Simon the Sorcerer had wanted to initiate—to take matters into his own hands, to buy the power, and to impart the power. He wanted everything to be his call and his decision. Peter said, in effect, "NO!" to Simon. He said:

> *"You can have no part in this, for your heart is not right with God"* (Acts 8:21).

His inner man, his heart, stood betrayed by his words. Consequently, he wasn't even allowed to take part in the ministry. He went from trying to be a "key player" to having no part at all. Simon's response to Peter touches my heart and shows that he quickly repented of his thoughts. His words?

> *"Pray to the LORD for me..."* (Acts 8:24).

Simon had been looking for a change in his life (receiving the power of the Holy Spirit) so that, he said, he might bless others. Peter diagnosed Simon's request as one full of jealousy. Simon seemed to want the abilities the other apostles had so that he could be like them. He didn't seem to have a longing for the indwelling, loving Presence of the Holy Spirit, Himself. If jealousy or pride or envy worms its way into our thoughts of ministry, we will surely find ourselves in opposition to the Spirit of Jesus. Our Lord, Jesus, was humble! In the Gospel of Matthew, Jesus says:

> ***"For even the Son of Man came not to be served but to serve others and to give his life as a ransom for many"*** (Matthew 20:28).

Motives matter! As we think about whether or not we're open to the communications of our Lord, our God, to us or to our world today, I think it's important to examine our own hearts and see if they reflect a receptive, humble spirit toward Him.

ONCE AGAIN, what are we asking of God?

Are we yearning for direction for ourselves or our congregations? Do we believe that the Holy Spirit is capable of giving us specific directions as to what to do?

Are we asking for that direction? Are we listening for it? Are we responding to it? OR do we make our own plans, set our own agendas, choose our own paths, and determine for ourselves who looks most approachable? Then, almost as an afterthought, do we ask the Lord to bless all of our own decisions?

How frightening to consider the words of Peter as if directed to me:

> *"You can have no part in this, for your heart is not right with God. Repent of your wickedness and pray to the LORD. Perhaps he will forgive your evil thoughts, for I can see that you are full of bitter jealousy and are held captive by sin"* (Acts 8:21–23).

If I'm wanting to be in control, if I'm wanting to be the initiator, if I want to impart the power, or if I think I possess the power to impart, I need to be forgiven for the thoughts in my heart.

Generally, it wasn't the bold and the self-confident who heard from the Lord and were used by Him. It was the unassuming and humble. Let's look to those examples as our guides.

The beginning of Acts 13 talks about certain prophets and teachers ministering to the Lord, praying and fasting, and being told by the Holy Spirit what to do (Acts 13:1). The Holy Spirit singled out Paul and Barnabas:

> *One day as these men were worshiping the LORD and fasting, the Holy Spirit said, "Appoint Barnabas and Saul for the special work to which I have called them"* (Acts 13:2).

Question: How did the Holy Spirit communicate to those prophets and teachers?

Answer: In Acts 13:2, we read "…the Holy Spirit said…" This choice of words indicates specific, spoken, communicated direction. Was it audible communication that the apostles heard with their ears, or was it thought communication? We aren't told, but the apostles clearly knew that the communication was from the Holy Spirit, and they acted upon it.

A number of years ago, I was "stuck" in a mental loop of frustration. My thoughts went something like this, *Oh dear! There is so much wrong with my life! There are so many things that need to be fixed! I know so many people who need so much help. I'm involved in relationships that need direction. Oh dear! There is so much wrong with my life! There are so many things that need to be fixed! I know so many people...e*tc.

One day, as I was driving to work, allowing the mental frustration list to loop and spin, a lone thought suddenly cut through all the chatter:

NAME ONE!

Where did THAT come from? I wondered. Nonetheless, that thought got my attention, and I decided to act on it. As soon as I began thinking through the specifics of my concerns, I quickly saw that some of my concerns were entirely out of my control. The only thing I could do for some of the situations was to pray, and I resolved to do just that. On one or two other fronts, a specific action came to mind that I COULD take to alleviate some of my frustrations, and I resolved to do those as well. In short, the "command" to get specific in naming my needs proved beyond just therapeutic. The specificity resolved the frustration. I identified the areas of concern for me, determined what, if any, action I could take, and then I took it!

Some time ago, as I was leaving a parking lot, I received an inaudible instruction within my head that said: *Get out and check the sides of your van.* I was anxious to get home and argued with the "thought." As I continued to drive another thought challenged me: *You've been praying for the courage to obey.* With that, I whipped my van into the first available parking space I could find and got out to "check" my sides. When I did, I found an unconscious woman in the car next to mine. I called 911 and the ambulance came and took her away. Coincidence? Absolutely not. I am wired for communication with my Lord, and He took advantage of it so I would help the woman.

Another time I received an inaudible communication within my head as I was passing in front of a man at church: *This man is not happy with his wife or with this church.* Within two weeks the man had left his wife and was filing for divorce. Coincidence? Absolutely not. I didn't even know the man except by name and his face. I had never had them into my home nor been into theirs. I am wired for communication with my Lord, and He took advantage of it so I would pray for this troubled man.

After the Presidential election of 2000, our nation was gripped for weeks in the unprecedented counting and recounting of ballots in the state of Florida. We learned of new words like "chads" and butterfly ballots. (Ballots were made of paper. People voted by punching out little areas next to the name of their candidate with an implement known as a stylus. Sometimes these areas weren't fully punched through and the paper that remained was called a "chad.") We heard daily on the news about some counties including "dimpled, pregnant, or hanging" chads in their vote count while other counties were not. Day after day, night after night I went to bed praying about the election. I prayed for my candidate to win, and I prayed for the voting tabulation to be consistent and fair. I was frustrated to the core with all the variations from county to county with vote tabulation. One night as I tossed in bed grumbling in my head about pregnant chads and dimpled chads and swinging chads these words came to my thoughts: *Yeah, it's Leviticus 19.*

"Yeah," I agreed, "Leviticus 19."

Then, suddenly, it hit me what I had just said: "Leviticus 19?? Where did THAT come from??"

Although I had read my Bible virtually all my life, I could NOT tell you even how many chapters Leviticus had let alone what the various chapters included. I knew that Leviticus had lots of laws in it, but I hadn't a clue what was where. I knew I may not remember the exact chapter by morning, and I knew this matter was important. So, I got out of bed, got my Bible, and began to read Leviticus 19, which covers a lot of territory. However, at the end of the chapter, the text states:

> *Do not use dishonest standards when measuring length, weight, or volume. Your scales and weights must be accurate. Your containers for measuring dry materials or liquids must be accurate. I am the LORD your God who brought you out of the land of Egypt* (Leviticus 19:35–36).

CONSISTENT STANDARDS!! God agreed with me!! Or, more accurately, I was reflecting teachings I had learned long ago from Him—His Holy Word—and He gave me book and chapter to validate my concerns.

This information was not a feeling or a sensation; it was a specific detail about a specific book in the Bible and a specific chapter of that book! I am wired for communication with my Father, and He let me know He supported my concerns.

I have talked with people who, like me, just suddenly KNEW something about someone they hadn't known before, nor would they have had any way of knowing. One day, a man, let's call him John, told me that God communicated to him that a particular brother, let's call him Bob, was engaging in a sin and needed to be confronted about it. God was specific with John and told him the exact sin in which Bob was engaged. God insisted John follow through with the confrontation of Bob. John obeyed. Bob immediately acknowledged the sin, and the two of them prayed for forgiveness and healing. A brother restored!! No one knew but God— and He wanted His son free from the evil of the plaguing sin.

A sister in Jesus shared with me that she heard God speak in an audible voice to her. She said she had been sitting on the back row in the auditorium where she worshipped. Suddenly, she heard a voice near her ear, somewhat behind her, say, "Call your brother." She turned around to see who was talking to her, and no one was there! She explained that she hadn't talked to nor even thought about her brother in years. She said she hadn't mentioned the fact that she even had a brother to anyone at her church. I believe there had been some sort of rift between them many years prior, and she was content to allow the rift to remain. God was not! So, she obediently got in touch with her brother, and a healed relationship resulted! The woman had gone into the church building to worship her heavenly Father. He, in turn, recognized an old wound and wanted to heal it properly. So, he communicated direction to her and she obeyed! Hallelujah!!

Question: When God decides to communicate with His children, what form does that communication take?

Answer: Any form He chooses!

A number of years ago I found myself posing all sorts of *"whys"* to God just in my own head. *Why, if what You want is spiritual connectedness to us, why did You bother making us into physical form? Why didn't You just create us as spiritual beings and be done with it? Why is this physical state necessary?* I quickly went on to point out to God some of the pitfalls of being human: *Humans can get hurt. We get sick, get diseased, we sometimes face disasters like tornadoes or hurricanes or earthquakes or floods or droughts or famine. We get cold, hot, thirsty, hungry. Some of us are born with physical or mental deficiencies. Some of us can't pay our bills or read a book or do math. And THEN there's the pain we inflict on one another—both emotional pain and physical pain. It's tough being a human.*

One day, after reading the newspaper and being overwhelmed with the pain and suffering in the world, I simply collapsed on my kitchen floor in one tearful heap, wondering, *Why? Why? Why?* I told God that I knew I sounded arrogant. After all, who was I to question the creator of the universe? I'm nothing. But, regardless of whether or not I had the right, I questioned His wisdom in making mankind. I received nothing from God. No immediate impression onto my brain. No comforting thought. No scripture leaped from my memory banks. Nothing. Total silence from the cosmos. Frustrated, I picked myself up and went about my daily chores.

It may have been that day, or the next that my little girl, Happy, came to me with a dilemma. Her elementary school fundraiser was due to be turned in the next day, but she hadn't collected all the money from the people who had ordered from her. I looked at the total due and realized that I could write a check to cover the cost, and then those who had ordered from her could simply pay me and all would be well. My very bright, very gifted little girl didn't get it. "But if YOU pay for everything, then it will all be YOURS, and then what will I tell the other people?" I explained the whole check writing, money reimbursing thing to her, but it was no good. The lights were off. She was stumped. Stuck. Frustrated.

Finally, I pulled my one ace out of the hole: her dependence on and trust in me. "Happy, who buys and prepares food for this family? Who takes care of the household needs? Who drives you where you need to go and takes care of you when you're sick? Haven't you learned that you can trust me? Well, even though you don't understand how all of this will work, can you just trust that I DO understand and I DO know what I'm talking about and it WILL work out okay??!!" Suddenly, in the middle of my explanation to my little girl, I realized that God was answering my question to Him through MY very own words coming out of MY very own mouth!!

It was as if God was saying:

> **Trust Me. I know you don't understand, but can you just trust Me—based on what you know about Me already—that I DO understand and it IS necessary for you, humans, to be in physical form for a while...**

That's all I needed. My heart leaped at the realization that HE had communicated to me in a way I could totally understand: through the simple communication of a parent to her child. I also understood that He wasn't disgusted with me! I had realized that even though my daughter was extremely bright, she simply hadn't had enough life experiences at that point to help her understand how reimbursing worked. Truthfully, I believed God, Himself, clouded her understanding just so we could have that entire conversation. Just as Happy didn't understand what I was proposing to do, I wasn't—and still am not—spiritually developed sufficiently to understand why a physical form is necessary. The bottom line, however, was trust. He was simply asking me if I would trust Him. My very, very full heart quickly responded "YES!"

Can God use our own words to teach, convict us? Of course He can!! He's God!!

Have you been asking God to communicate to you? Are you truly listening for Him to speak to you? And, are you willing to acknowledge that communication? Are you willing to act on any message you receive?

When my oldest child was in kindergarten, she opted to take her first pulled tooth into the classroom for show and tell. We put the tooth into a baggie, the baggie into her back pack, and the back pack onto her back. Then out the door she ran and jumped into our friend's car for the carpool to school. When I went to pick her up at the end of the day, my little broken-hearted angel came running to me with tears streaming down her face: "Oh Mommy!" she sobbed. "I lost it!!," she said, referring to her tooth. Poor little girl. I tried soothing her on our drive to drop off the friend's child, but she was inconsolable.

"Mommy! Please take me back to look for it!"

What's a mom to do? I dropped off the little boy, turned the car around and took my daughter back to her classroom. When we entered, her teacher took one look at us and knew immediately why we were there. She quipped, "We looked for it! We really did. But there's so much rice on the floor from our craft project today that we kept mistaking rice for the tooth. So, we quit."

She was willing to allow us to stay in the classroom and look anyway, but she needed to leave. She simply asked that we close the door and turn off the lights when we left.

My daughter and I got down on the floor and looked. Yep, rice. Everywhere. AND, the floor tiles were white with black specks to begin with.

I moaned.

"Lauren, we're going to need to pray for God's help with this one." We were down on the floor anyway, I figured it was an easy segue.

We prayed. Then, I'm not sure if I heard or simply detected that someone was at the door. I looked up and saw another teacher standing in the doorway looking questioningly at us.

I began to explain, "Oh, we're looking for my daughter's lost tooth. She brought it in for show and tell today, but she lost it."

Then, in the next instant, I sensed the Lord encouraging: *Acknowledge what you were doing.*

HUH? I countered, *But the teacher might think I'm nuts! Acknowledge what you were doing.*

Still on the floor, without rising, I quipped, "so we're just throwing up a little prayer here to help us find it."

Her expression didn't change as she simply grunted, "uh-huh." Then she added, "just close the door and turn off the lights when you leave."

Yep, I thought, *she thinks I'm nuts.*

Lauren and I looked through her book bag again as well and that's when I noticed a hole. Ah-ha! I asked Lauren if she had taken the tooth out to show her friend on the ride to school. Yes! She did!

"Okay, Lauren!" I announced with great assurance in my tone, "I believe I know where you tooth is! I think it must have fallen out in the car on your way to school this morning. We'll go ask if we can look through the car and I'm pretty sure we'll find it in there."

Poor little girl wasn't convinced. We turned off the lights and closed the door and walked down the hallway hand in hand. We both felt a little sad. She was mourning the loss of her lost tooth, and I think, more than anything, I was mourning another blow to my pride.

I pushed open one of the many doors that lead out of the school onto the sidewalk. We stepped out, looked down and THERE IT WAS!! THE TOOTH!! Lauren's lost tooth!!

I yelped and bent over to pick it up. Even as I did so, I received another communication from my Lord. I understood Him to say, *The moment you acknowledged your need for Me was when I determined to let you find the tooth.*

Oh reader! Please don't skim over this part! Our Heavenly Father is INTIMATELY aware of your every thought and concern. A tooth, Mary?? YES!! Even a tooth. Think of this: hundreds and hundreds of little feet had walked, stumbled, and run out of those doors that day. But my Lord knew exactly where to position that tooth and which door to have me push open so I could find it. And what did He want from me? I believe He just wanted me to grow in my faith. Simply by acknowledging to another human that I needed Him required a squelching of my pride. He KNEW the reward would be HUGE, but I needed to learn and grow. Pride needed to go. Communication. Wow!

Praise You, Lord, Jesus!! You made the lame walk, the blind see, the proud to be humbled—and You led me right to my little girl's tooth! Thank You!

Chapter Three

WHAT HAPPENS WHEN WE RECEIVE OR REJECT GOD'S COMMUNICATION TO US?

I want to consider those people who don't sense God communicating to them in their thoughts. Is that you? Perhaps, after studying the scriptures, earnestly and honestly, you're part of a group who believe that God doesn't communicate with us anymore except through His written Word.

I've known a number of people who meet that description. They look at 1 Corinthians 13:8–12 for biblical support. Those passages deal with certain manifestations of the Spirit ceasing when the "perfect" comes. Within my own particular former church, there were many who believed that the "perfect" is the written Word: the canonization (or scholarly agreed upon acceptance of which writings were to be incorporated into the Holy Bible.) The thinking was that when all the writings of the New Testament were put into book form, a perfect explanation of the life and teachings of Jesus had become available to mankind and supernatural manifestations were no longer necessary. The written word was all that was needed.

A passage in 1 Corinthians says:

> *Now we see things imperfectly, like puzzling reflections in a mirror, but then we will see everything with perfect clarity. All that I know now is partial and incomplete, but then I will know everything completely, just as God now knows me completely* (1 Corinthians 13:12).

Many people reason that Paul meant that he didn't yet have access to the full written testimonies of the other apostles or disciples. However, when all the inspired writers penned their writings, then knowledge would be complete and spiritual manifestations—

prayed-for-miracles, prophesy, words of knowledge, speaking in unknown tongues, etc.—would cease.

I am not a scholar. I am not a theologian. Maybe that's why I don't know fully. But, frankly, I've never met anyone who was a scholar or a theologian who I thought knew fully either! I've known scholars and theologians who could rip a text apart and put it back together again seamlessly, but who didn't seem to have a clue as to how to get along with their coworkers. Since Paul talks in verse 13 of chapter 13 in 1st Corinthians about love being the greatest spiritual manifestation, doesn't it follow that to know fully would prompt an understanding/knowledge of loving fully? AND wouldn't Paul want us to DO it?

Receiving Communication from God

But, the real reason that I DON'T BELIEVE that the spiritual manifestations have stopped has nothing to do with scholarship or theology. The reason I believe spiritual manifestations happen today is because **I keep experiencing them.**

I'm told that an individual with a scientific bent once approached Hall of Fame Baseball pitcher Dizzy Dean and explained to him, scientifically, how a "curve" ball, or throwing a ball that curved, was simply an impossibility. Dizzy reportedly said to him, "You can tell me all you want that I don't throw a curve ball, but let me invite you to go stand on the other side of that tree where I can't see you, and I'll throw this ball and hit you with it, and then we'll discuss whether or not my ball curves!"

That experiential certainty is how it is with those of us who are aware of the activity of the Holy Spirit in our lives. When the scholars and the theologians stand up and begin their rhetoric of how the Spirit is no longer active, we begin to dismiss ourselves from the audience. It's time for a break, or a drink, or whatever. Typically we wander around and innocently bump into one another. Coincidence? That's when the sharing takes place. "I know he doesn't believe the Spirit is active anymore, but I really had an interesting experience last week..." Then another shares, and another and another. This sequence of events has happened to me time and time again.

At the church where we worshipped when I was a young woman, I don't recall hearing about anyone having had an "experience" with the Holy Spirit other than being convicted of sin, or feeling God's love and forgiveness for them. I was certainly encouraged to love God and was fortunate to have been taught by many, many precious people who I knew loved God AND me! Consequently, I felt connected to God and was very open to receiving communication from Him. Little by little, I began picking up books written by those who also believed they had received some kind of communication from God. How well do I remember reading David Wilkerson's *The Cross and the Switchblade*. It thrilled my soul. I had always known God wanted to communicate and be active and powerful in our lives as

He was in Mr. Wilkerson's life, but I had never known anyone who responded to His nudges as did Mr. Wilkerson.

I determined to keep my heart open to the nudges of God. I yearned to be led by Him. I prayed. However, I continued to worship at a church that rarely spoke of being Spirit led or "filled with the Spirit" or communicated to by God. At one point, after I had married, my husband and I met with an elder and his wife and asked them about our sense of wanting more from God. We asked them about the spiritual manifestations mentioned in 1 Corinthians 12. How well I remember listening to the elder's wife say, "You all are so far above that! You don't need that!" I guess she looked at the spiritual manifestations as crutches. All I remember thinking was, *You don't know me at all! I need them desperately!*

*SURELY NO ONE WANTS TO QUENCH THE HOLY SPIRIT, BUT…*I, however, continued to want the leaders of the church where I worshipped to approve of or even recognize my interest in and hunger for teachings of The Holy Spirit and His leading/interacting with us today. Sadly, I was not encouraged or offered information to satisfy that hunger.

At one point, during the weekly ladies' Bible study that met at our church, I began thinking out loud about spiritual gifts as mentioned in 1 Corinthians 12. That passage reads:

> *A spiritual gift is given to each of us so we can help each other. To one person the Spirit gives the ability to give wise advice to another the same Spirit gives a message of special knowledge. The same Spirit gives great faith to another, and to someone else the one Spirit gives the gift of healing. He gives one person the power to perform miracles, and another the ability to prophesy. He gives someone else the ability to discern whether a message is from the Spirit of God or from another spirit. Still another person is given the ability to speak in unknown languages, while another is given the ability to interpret what is being*

said. It is the one and only Spirit who distributes all these gifts. He alone decides which gift each person should have (1 Corinthians 12:7–11).

I shared that I was curious about why I hadn't seen any miracles nor been around anyone with the power to heal the sick. Yet, scriptures are consistent.

Jesus Christ is the same yesterday, today, and forever (Hebrews 13:8).

At that, one of the women, a major leader of the group, simply added, "I'm surprised you don't look at Romans 12. There's a wonderful list of spiritual manifestations there, and we see them all the time!"

In his grace, God has given us different gifts for doing certain things well. So if God has given you the ability to prophesy, speak out with as much faith as God has given you. If your gift is serving others, serve them well. If you are a teacher, teach well. If your gift is to encourage others, be encouraging. If it is giving, give generously. If God has given you leadership ability, take the responsibility seriously. And if

94

*you have a gift for showing kindness to others,
do it gladly* (Romans 12:6–8).

At that, ANOTHER woman spoke up, sighing, and simply said, "I just want to study the Bible, Mary. I just want to follow the Bible."

I had ONLY been READING THE BIBLE to them. However, the women knew that not everyone believed that the Lord continues to communicate with us today, as in the past, through the above mentioned gifts (1 Corinthians 12). They were nervous of controversy. So, wanting to be peace keepers, they opted to "move on." No miracles. No gifts of healing. No special knowledge.

A number of years later, my husband David and I decided to meet with a church that was very open to the presence of the Holy Spirit. The church was large, so, to get better acquainted, we broke up into smaller "getting to know you" groups throughout the week. We had visited one of these smaller groups once and were visiting a second time. Just as we were about to get out of our car to go into the house, I saw a woman entering who I hadn't noticed the previous time. She stood out. She was wearing what looked like Mickey Mouse ears on her head.

There may have been a dozen of us in the living room of our host. The man spoke up and simply said something to the effect of us each being welcome to share a song or a scripture or a prayer or a word of knowledge or anything we sensed the Lord putting into our hearts to share. That simple invitation blessed me immensely. I'd never heard such a sweet invitation to be open to communication from and to our Lord. So simple. So refreshing.

CONTACT from the Holy Spirit:
A Word of Knowledge!!

THEN IT HAPPENED. The woman who'd been wearing the Mickey Mouse ears, addressed David and me. (She had removed the ears by now.) She said something like, "David and Mary, I believe the Lord would like me to tell you that He's aware you're carrying around a great burden of disappointment. I believe He wants me to tell you He's ready to lift that disappointment and replace the years the locusts have eaten with joy!"

David and I smiled. Sweet. Not earth shattering, but encouraging. Our first "word of knowledge," or "special knowledge" imparted to us from the Lord.

Others shared. We prayed, sang, read scripture, and after twenty or thirty minutes, the host concluded our time together in prayer. Snack time! It was during snack time that this same woman who'd had the word of knowledge from the Lord came up to me and said something like, "I know I said the word was for both you and David, Mary, but I really think it was more for you. Mary, the picture I have is that the disappointment inside you is like great shards of glass around your heart. Nothing comes into you unless it comes through the glass and nothing goes out of you unless it goes through the glass. What is it, Mary? What has caused you so much disappointment??"

All I could do was stare at her. What had caused me disappointment? I mumbled something like, "I can't tell you."

She smiled and reminded me, "Well, the Lord plans to replace it with joy anyway!"

I walked away wondering. Disappointment? Great shards of glass? I hadn't said ANYTHING in the group about anything—let alone about disappointment. What made her think I was disappointed in anything? Then I recalled what she'd said: "Nothing comes in and nothing goes out unless it passes through the glass—the disappointment."

Quickly, I decided to think about something and see what disappointment popped into my mind.

Methodically, I went about thinking about my children. David and I had four. One had just finished college. One was in his second year of college. One was finishing high school, and one was beginning high school.

Revelation! Over and over, as I thought about my children, I discovered I wasn't disappointed in ANY of them. But I WAS disappointed. Majorly disappointed. Disappointed in myself!! My children were doing GREAT, but my thoughts were all about how I'd failed them. I wasn't the mother I should have been. I didn't love enough or laugh enough or support enough or…on and on. Never enough. Ugh.

Then I had another thought: *What is disappointment rooted in? Was my disappointment just rooted in disappointment? Or was there something else, underneath all that disappointment?* Gently, ever so gently, my heavenly Father began to reveal truth to me. Disappointment in my failures was rooted in my pride. I looked back on my parenting skills—or lack of them—and moaned. Then it hit me. I had wanted others to look at me as if I had it all together, but I didn't! There I'd been, trying to sit on some kind of throne I'd envisioned for myself, but no one could bow before me because I didn't deserve it, and I couldn't even bow to myself!

Hey! Wait! What was I doing on the throne?? I loved Jesus! I wanted JESUS to be on the throne of my heart!! So, with my head bowed, I imagined myself sliding off the throne as I asked Jesus to please forgive me and kindly sit on the throne of my heart instead. I think I saw Him smile as He sat.

Why do I share that story? Because, dear reader, that word of knowledge, that communication from God on that one night in the living room of a man I'd only met once, spoken by a woman (A mom—just like me—except she wore Mickey Mouse ears to a prayer meeting, for goodness sake!) whom I'd never met before, changed my life!! From that day on, whenever Satan would remind me of my failures as a wife, mother, homemaker, sister, daughter, on and on and on, I could inwardly retort, *You know, you're right! I'm a LOSER! But Lord JESUS redeemed me! He Loves Me! He paid the penalty for all my mistakes!! And He BOUGHT me!!*

He owns me!! If you have anything bad to say about me, you'll have to go to HIM! Good luck with that! It didn't work out too well for you the last time!! HALLELUJAH!! I am loved, Jesus is on the throne and all is well!!

Yep, Jesus replaced the disappointment with joy. One word of knowledge—and the power of my mighty Savior—did that.

Nudges, Signs, and Warnings

On another day, I recall going about my normal routine, when the name of a friend, whom I hadn't seen in a while, popped into my head. I thought it curious, but I continued whatever it was I had been doing. Then, the name popped into my head again. And again. I thought that was curious. Then, I was driving my car and BOOM! There was the name again! That time I decided the Lord must want me to pay attention! So, I did. I called her. I asked her how she was doing and she, cheerfully, it seemed to me, quipped "Oh, I'm fine, Mary. How are you?" I told her I was well, but that her name had been coming into my head for the past few days, and I felt the Lord was encouraging me to call her and remind her that He loved her and He was very aware of all she was going through. (I, on the other hand, hadn't a clue.) At that, she gasped and began to cry. She told me that her best friend had passed away just a few days previously, and she'd been devastated. She said she'd been walking around her house crying out, "God, do you HEAR me?? Do you even CARE that my heart is breaking?? I NEED TO HEAR FROM YOU!!" My phone call was the confirmation her aching heart desperately needed. A child of God was comforted and reassured.

On another occasion, I was walking through my bedroom when I looked down on the floor and there, looking up at me, was an envelope encasing a letter from an old friend. Where had THAT come from?? I hadn't been reading old letters. I had no memory of having seen that letter in ages. Still, it was right in the middle of the floor! That could NOT have "just" happened. So, I decided to give the family a call. David and I had been friends with both the husband and the wife when we'd lived in the same town. Then we all moved. Afterwards, we'd visited in their home—out of state—and they'd visited in ours. I called and found that their number had changed. No worries. He'd been the pastor of their local church. I decided to phone the church and ask for the family's new number. Hmm. The secretary confirmed that my friends had actually moved out of state and taken a new job. Graciously, she gave me their new number.

I dialed the number and immediately recognized my male friend's voice. I immediately gave him my name and said I hoped he didn't mind that I'd tracked him/them down. We laughed and then I jumped in with both feet. I told him about the strange coincidence with the letter in the middle of the floor. Once again, I said something like, "I believe the Lord wanted me to call you to let you know He loves you and He's very aware of all you've been going through. Obviously, with the change in states and churches, you've been going through a whole lot. I believe He wants you to know that you are not alone. He knows exactly what has happened and He loves you." At that, my very strong, very godly friend, began to weep. He managed to say that he couldn't talk but simply added that I could have no idea how much my phone call meant to him.

A hurting child of God, needing some sort of tangible confirmation from his heavenly Father, received it. What a blessing to be a tool in the hand of our loving God!

Conversely, had I not called, had I not yielded to God's nudges, what might have happened? I'll never know. God MIGHT have used someone else to encourage my friends, but what if they didn't listen, either?? A LOT of discouraged people are out there. Why is that? Have some of us been receiving nudges to convey God's love only to quench those nudges and say, "NO!" How many others could have been comforted or corrected or rescued by one simple call saying "I believe the Lord would like me to share this with you—"

Although this book is being written to encourage each of us to listen and attempt to obey the nudges we believe we receive from our Lord, it's also an opportunity for me to acknowledge some of my own resistance to those nudges. I recall a time when I was in an airport, going through a line to purchase something to eat. The clerk told me the price of what I was buying, but, for some reason, my brain went into slow motion and I simply could not manage to get the money out of my wallet with any speed at all. The man behind me, clearly frustrated, quipped, "it isn't that hard." Instantly, I felt the need to say to him, "And THAT is precisely the attitude that has brought about the rift between you and your son!" Did I say it? No. Why? Well, I reasoned that I didn't know the man. I also didn't even know if he HAD a son, let alone if they had a rift. But, as I've thought back on that moment, contemplating how he MIGHT have responded or what else the Holy Spirit may have prompted me to say if I had spoken up, I've wondered: Had the Holy Spirit meant for our encounter to be the beginning of a healing between the man and his son? Was our meeting to have promoted a better relationship between the man and God? Of course, I'll never know. I DO know that my Lord has forgiven me, but I confess to being sad that I let that opportunity pass me by.

Even if you've formerly resisted a nudge from the Lord, could you entertain the possibility that He might be trying to communicate to someone, using YOU as His tool?? Will you at least pray to try to be open to Him??

OR perhaps that nudge will be for you to take care of YOU! On one occasion, as I was driving down the road on my way home, the thought came to me, "The man in the car behind you is following you. Don't go home." WHAT?? I hadn't even noticed that there was a car behind me. I tried not to overreact. My own self-preservation kicked in, and I decided not to tip him off that I was aware of him. I casually glanced into my rear-view mirror. No eye contact. I just checked his car. Oh, it was a truck. He wasn't too close. Nothing at all abnormal. Still, the knot in the pit of my stomach was tightening.

What was going on?? I had just left the home of a sweet friend. We'd talked about life, our children, meal planning, etc., etc., etc. Nothing remotely frightening. Yet, I was confident the alert I'd just received was to be taken seriously. My Father had just communicated to me that I was in a potentially dangerous spot. I needed to be wise.

What should I do? The police station wasn't too far from where I was, but the man hadn't actually done anything. I could run by the grocery store…but then what? He could be waiting. There were only two more roads to turn onto and then I'd be home. What should I do?? Suddenly it entered my mind that there was a gated community very near my home. That was it! I could try to see if my friend Marie was home and could lift the gate for me! I pulled into the entrance to that community and the truck pulled up to the entrance without actually pulling into the driveway. He remained parallel to the street. There were no other cars around. He seemed to be waiting.

I entered the side marked "guests." There was a phone pad where I typed in her number and, if she answered, she could press a button that would lift the "gate" at my entrance. "Please, Lord," I prayed, "let her be at home and hear the phone!" Almost immediately, I heard her sweet greeting. Upon hearing my name she quipped, "You get on in here!" and lifted that gate!!! THANK YOU, GOD!!

I looked back and saw that the driver of the truck now pulled his truck into the entrance as well. I didn't stick around to see anything else. Did he happen to know anyone in the community he could call to be admitted? Would he try to con his way in with one of the security guards? I never found out. I didn't break the speed laws of the community, but I was no slowpoke, either. I reached Marie's home, quickly went inside and breathed a sweet sigh of relief. My Lord had protected me. He alerted me, I listened, took the necessary precautions, and I was safe.

On another occasion, a "friend," came to visit in our home. On this particular morning, David wasn't home. The plan had been that our friend would leave for a conference early in the morning—shortly after David left for work. But, he didn't leave. He wanted to talk. So, we sat at my dining room table and talked. His heart was full and he began to cry. Suddenly, I received a clear spiritual impression: *DO NOT GET UP TO GIVE THAT MAN A HUG OR COMFORT HIM.* I sat, with my arms folded, leaned back in my chair and listened to the man for a few more minutes. Inwardly, I assured, *Don't you worry, Lord. I won't.* The man calmed down and, after a few more minutes, left for the conference. I'll never know what was going on inside that man on that day, but, I confess, I never felt comfortable around him again.

Sadly, I have known of other women who have told me of times when they just "knew" that they shouldn't be alone with a person, but they dismissed it. "Something told me I wasn't going to be safe with him," but they'd reasoned that thought away: "No, he's a good guy. He's kind to me." They concluded they were just being silly. Then something horrific happened. I've actually heard and read of advice now being given to women that goes something like, "If something inside you tells you that you aren't safe with a person, DON'T GO WITH HIM/HER. Trust your gut!" Gut. HA!! God uses His Spirit and, yes, even angels to communicate to humans. If we "feel it" in our guts, then okay! That's a start! How many people could have been saved from serious trauma if they'd only listened to that inner voice??

If we aren't aware of the spiritual realm all around us, if we only think it's "us" and nothing more, then we use our logic. Logic didn't save me when the Lord told me a man was following me, nor did it help when our "friend" stayed too long. The Holy Spirit did.

Abortion: a Symbol

Many years ago, I decided to take a stand against abortion: the termination of a baby's life while still in the womb. I am pro-life and I began supporting pro-life groups. I marched on Washington. Several years ago, I volunteered to help out in our local pro-life office. I would answer the telephone if it rang. We took turns staffing the office. When it was my turn, I was the only one in the office. After letting myself into the office and logging in, I discovered that I couldn't sit at the desk and simply wait for phone calls. Neither could I clean shelves or do much of anything. I felt compelled to pray. All I could do inside that little office was pray—and pace. I'd start to sit down and then pop right back up again. It was as if the spirit within me was letting me know that "this" was urgent! No time for sitting. Pray! Pray! Pray! So, I prayed and paced. Prayed and paced, prayed and paced. It was a little office, no larger than twelve or fifteen square feet. The room was packed with reading material, filing cabinets, shelves, and a desk. There wasn't a large amount of room for pacing, but I managed. Day after day, time after time, I let myself into the room, sat down at the desk and then stood up to pray and pace.

My prayers, which I prayed out loud, were always the same: "Dear Lord, please stop these abortions! Please open the eyes of the people. Let them see that this is wrong! Please turn the hearts of the people away from this horrible evil. Please allow mothers to see that the children growing within them aren't meant to hurt or lessen their enjoyment in life but to ENHANCE it!! Dear God, please stop abortion!!"

One day, as I was going through this prayer, pointing out to God that in the briefest moment He could alter some "switch" in the minds of abortion activists and they could see that abortion was bad, it was at that point that a disturbing thought came to me:

WHAT HAPPENS WHEN WE RECEIVE OR REJECT GOD'S COMMUNICATION TO US?

Abortion is a symbol.

Symbol? I questioned. *What symbol?*

Abortion is symbolic of what the church is doing to My Holy Spirit.

This thought nearly terrified me. The implications were staggering. Could it be? Was this thought truly from Jehovah God? Had the Holy Spirit actually conveyed a spiritual truth to me that was well known within the heavenly, spiritual realms? Did Satan believe that he had the right to lay claim to the lives of innocent physical babies because God's people, the church, were aborting the very spiritual Presence of God within them?

I came home and shared this "insight" with my husband. He wasn't convinced it was from God. "But the church is the body of Christ. It does a lot of good." He thought people would assume I was blaming the church for abortions. What I believe the Lord communicated to me is that Christians won't be able to turn this nation against abortions until we stop resisting the activity of the Holy Spirit within our own lives and within the church as a whole. The thought, *Abortion is a symbol of what the church is doing to My Holy Spirit,* was chilling, but the impression I had was that God is allowing abortion to continue until Christians wake up to the horrific, deadly, vile wrong of quenching or aborting the nudges or the activity of the Holy Spirit within us. I'm aware that the vast majority of us in the church think abortion is WRONG! We're the ones who write articles, pray, contribute money, pray, support unwed mothers, adopt babies, pray, offer counseling to those experiencing post-abortion syndrome, pray. We're NOT an evil group!! Abortion is evil!

If the Holy Spirit desires to bring about activity which we refuse to allow, isn't that an abortion?

If the Holy Spirit desires to bless us by "giving birth" to events which we fear or don't see the worth of and stifle, isn't this an abortion?

WHAT HAPPENS WHEN WE RECEIVE OR REJECT GOD'S COMMUNICATION TO US?

If He desires to express Himself in a particular way but we say "He no longer manifests Himself in (such and such) way," isn't that an abortion?

The scriptures say, ***"Don't quench"*** (or extinguish—like a fire) ***"the Holy Spirit"*** (1 Thessalonians 5:19).

The Holy Spirit is the Spirit of God. God is love (1 John 4:8). God is life (John 1:4). Both love and life are active. Neither love nor life is stagnant. Life is not always predictable. Life can throw us curves. Sometimes we start off in one direction and end up going completely opposite of where we were headed. We cannot predict the Holy Spirit. We can, according to Paul, however, restrict the Holy Spirit's activity in our lives (1 Thessalonians 5:19).

When a woman is pregnant, her unborn baby poses an abundance of changes and possibilities for her: her figure will change—some might find her unattractive (some might find her MORE attractive!); her ability to remain employed may change—she may need to quit work; she may undergo emotional changes—she may need help in order to cope with the new stresses and demands of caring for a child; she may receive more love than she ever thought possible; she may discover that being needed is one of the greatest joys in life; she may discover talents within her she never suspected; she may discover resources from within and without that will sustain her for the remainder of her life. The possibilities of growth because of motherhood are limitless!! BUT if she aborts the child, she will never know what "might" have been. Why would a woman abort her child? Fear seems to be at the root.

2 Timothy 3:5, which we looked at earlier, refers to characteristics of some people in the "last days." They will be lovers of self, lovers of money, boastful, arrogant, revilers, and, among other things, "hold to a form of godliness, although they have denied its power." Is that us? Have we denied, do we deny the power of the Holy Spirit? If so, why? Why deny power from God?

WHAT HAPPENS WHEN WE RECEIVE OR REJECT GOD'S COMMUNICATION TO US?

In a word: fear. We're no different than a woman with child. Where should a child be the most safe? In the womb of the mother. The child knows no fear, no pain, no sorrow. He doesn't know cold or hot. He's comfortable. He's welcome. He's wanted. He's anticipated with joy. At least, he should be. But, when a woman decides to abort her child, she generally does so because her fears have overpowered her: What if I'm no longer attractive? What if I lose my job? What if I can't cope emotionally? What if we don't have enough money to send another child to college? Fear wins and a child—full of possibility and promise—is aborted.

I believe some people in the church view the Holy Spirit no differently than how some pregnant women think of their unborn child. Please read on as I attempt to draw comparisons between the two.

Where should the Holy Spirit be most welcome, most wanted? In the church! In the lives of individual Christians! He should be anticipated with joy. He should know He's welcome, wanted, expected.

However, when we don't talk about Him, or anticipate His activity, His involvement in our lives are we not ignoring our power source? When He attempts to get our attention and we pay no attention to Him, aren't we neglecting, even quenching the Spirit? My precious mother once put it this way: "We treat the Holy Spirit like an unwanted step-child!"

Why would we treat the Holy Spirit so badly? Our fearful thoughts continue: *What if He puts it on our heart to do something out of the ordinary? Will I look silly? Will people think of me as a kook? Will I be considered some kind of religious whacko?* Those feelings may have started in fear, but they keep going because of self-love, arrogance. and pride.

> **They will act as if they are religious, but they will reject the power that could make them godly** (2nd Timothy 3:5).

A number of years ago, I was in earnest prayer for my little nephew who had been struggling with leukemia for six years. Day after day I spoke out loud

118

as I prayed, "Lord, please heal Bobby!" One day I prayed, "Lord, are you listening? I've been praying for a long time now, and even though he goes in and out of remission, he hasn't been healed yet. I need for You to heal him!" A thought came to me, *What will you do if I heal him?* Very quickly I responded *I WILL PRAISE YOU!!* Then another thought came: *What will you do if I allow him to die?* That was a miserable moment. I thought about stomping my foot and walking away from God as I wondered: *Why encourage us to ask You for stuff if You're just going to tell us no??!!*

Still the question was on the table...What would I do if God allowed Bobby to die? I thought again about walking away. Where would I go? I didn't understand why He might say "no" but I had walked with Him long enough to know that He, ultimately, IS good. He really IS loving and kind and merciful. I had experienced His love too many times to deny it. Finally, very slowly, I admitted that if He allowed my nephew to die, although I wouldn't like it, I would still honor and praise Him.

Then, continued the thought, *Why don't you start right now?* Immediately the scripture, **"This is the day the LORD has made; Let us rejoice and be glad in it,"** (Psalm 118:24), came to mind. I said it out loud. I felt that the Lord was teaching me that EVERY day is HIS day and HE is worthy to be praised in it whether or not I like what I see in it. So I praised and I smiled and I felt encouraged. He might allow Bobby to die or He might allow Bobby to live. But whatever happened, my role was to praise God—regardless!

Then I had another thought: *Wouldn't that verse be a great way to answer the phone?*

YES! I inwardly exclaimed. *After all, the phone rings in the privacy of my own home. They're calling me. They're on MY turf. They've "invaded" MY space. I get to say whatever I want in my home, in my space. I can praise God and bring glory to God right here in my living room whenever the phone rings! I'll do it!!*

WHAT HAPPENS WHEN WE RECEIVE OR REJECT GOD'S COMMUNICATION TO US?

This was truly a wonderful, exhilarating moment. I was confident! I was enthusiastic! I was rejoicing. Then reality hit. The phone rang.

Immediately a war began to rage within me. "Say it, Mary, say it" counseled the quiet, steady voice.

"ARE YOU NUTS??!" the other, harsher voice said. "If people THOUGHT you were a bit "off" before, now they're certainly going to think you've lost it if you start quoting scripture on the telephone!!"

I walked to the phone with my insides in turmoil—the quiet voice and the strident one. Both advising, both with merit. I picked up the phone and brought it to my ear and mouth, still uncertain as to which side would win. Not until I opened my mouth and actually heard the word "hello" come out of me, did I know which side would win. Upon saying the one word of greeting, an enormous wave of regret washed over me—I'd missed an opportunity. Then, before the wave could crash, I listened more intently as the voice at the

OTHER end of the line said "This is the day that the Lord has made. Let us rejoice and be glad in it!"

I quickly learned that my good friend Maurine had been praying for me that morning as she had been doing her housework. She said, "It was the strangest thing. I was vacuuming when all of a sudden I had the strongest urge to go to the phone, call you and give you a scripture. I didn't even know what I was supposed to say until I heard your voice, then I knew exactly what I was supposed to say. Why?"

Methods of Rejection—That Enemy Called Pride

Did I quench the Spirit? Yes I did. Why? Because He had been encouraging me to proclaim my confidence in God to the caller but I was afraid of looking/sounding naïve, silly. Had He truly given me the idea? I'm confident He did—after all, my friend quoted to me the very scripture I'd been wrestling with at the very time I'd been wrestling. Her response was not coincidence—it was definitely God's intervention.

WHAT HAPPENS WHEN WE RECEIVE OR REJECT GOD'S COMMUNICATION TO US?

He'd been listening to all my prayers. He confirmed to me that He'd been listening. Did He have something wonderful planned if I had been faithful on the telephone? I won't know until I reach Heaven. I'm almost afraid to ask. I know I've been forgiven for not answering the phone correctly that time—but I also have to live with the knowledge that I did quench the Spirit within me. That kind of error has caused me to pray to be obedient when the Spirit nudges me. I'm not saying it's any easier. I still wrestle with pride and love of self. Nonetheless, I don't want to quench the Spirit. I WANT to obey.

None of us knows what battles are being fought in the heavenly realms—nor do we know how they are happening. We're simply told not to quench the Spirit. We ARE told that our battles on Earth are not with flesh and blood, but in the spiritual realm—where thoughts are known and fears are catalogued. We are told in Ephesians 6:12 that we'll be engaged in battle against the rulers of the darkness of this world, against spiritual hosts of wickedness in heavenly places. The devil is active. He monitors thoughts too. In my situation with the caller at that time, the devil knew to come at me with fear and pride as he said: "You don't want to look/sound stupid, Mary! What will people say??" Fear and pride were and are powerful tools of his that trip me up more often than I want to admit. And THAT SITUATION was in the privacy of my own home! In the church, among brothers and sisters—where we should all be safe—we've also learned to fear. Wanting the approval of man has robbed me of witnessing my Lord's power through me in the past. But, unless I'm very vigilant, unless WE are vigilant, wanting approval can and will pull our eyes off our Lord and onto ourselves and our pride time and time again. Let's be very, very prayerful, family of God.

Speaking of the family of God, when I was a little girl and went to Sunday morning services, the women wore dresses and high heels, and the men wore coats and ties. It was important to look right! My own mother, who loved the Lord dearly, often explained that we had dressed up to show respect to the Lord. I realize Sunday attire has largely changed at this point, although I'm sure there are places where dresses, coats, and ties are still preferred. Yet though the acceptable attire is, largely, "casual," I believe there are still "norms" that most people try to follow. The key is that we want to look right to our fellow man. It's pride. God knows it and so does Satan.

No one wants to look silly—well, actually, some people make their living looking and acting silly—but even THAT ACTIVITY is pride based. If the silliness doesn't receive the proper amount of laughs or at least laughter from the right people, then even the planned silliness falls short and leaves the actor disappointed. The point is that pride is a serious villain—even in the church.

When we enter the building, the gathering spot for those who love Jesus, we're immediately confronted with the visual thing: Do we all fit the proper look?

From there, we're usually guided into a room for study or into the auditorium for corporate worship. Usually someone "presides" over the assembly and directs the study or the conversation or the worship service. Rarely is there any opportunity for anything spontaneous to happen. Most of us like organization. Some of us pretend not to, but it makes us feel secure. We generally like to know what to expect. I've talked with people who worshipped with those who never planned anything prior to assembling on Sunday morning. "It was chaos, Mary. The song leader would stand up front and fumble for which song to lead. Someone would read a scripture, and we all just hoped that whoever spoke would have thought it through first!"

And so it goes. Some of us think our services are too organized. Others seem to regard any change in the norm as being a slide into heresy. Some of us like to dress casually; others believe a coat and tie is the proper Sunday morning attire. And surrounding us all is the Holy Spirit wanting to communicate the thoughts of the Father to us. If someone in blue jeans was to stand up in the assembly on Sunday morning and proclaim something he/she was certain the Holy Spirit had put on his/her heart, the individuals who supported "suits and dresses only for Sunday a.m. attire" might be inclined to dismiss any comments from such a one as being inconsequential.

"How am I supposed to take him seriously? Just look at him!" (Conversely, if someone walked into a casual-attire crowd wearing dress-up threads, he might be looked down on for the same reason.) Likewise, the one who favored a well-planned program might regard any type of spontaneous proclamation as out of order and rude. The blessing of the sharing would have been lost because the biases of those assembled simply could not accommodate anything outside of their own parameters of acceptability.

How is the Father to get through to us? For some, the "look" is, if not credential itself, certainly representative of credentials. For others, it is form, decorum, correct speech AT the correct time that dictates whether or not one is to be heard and, once heard, heeded.

How is the Father to get through to us?

If the bath water lacks the bubbles or the proper temperature, OUT it goes! If the baby was in it at the time—poor baby!!

How is the Father to get through to us?

I believe it is this same fear of ridicule or failure that figures into both the decision of the pregnant woman to abort her child, and to the Christian to abort the leading of the Holy Spirit. Please consider comparing the possible thinking of a pregnant woman toward the child within her to the thinking of a Christian being encouraged to share something like a "word of knowledge" on Sunday morning.

Pregnant woman: "How can I take care of this baby? I can barely take care of myself!"

Christian: "What makes me think they'll listen to anything I say? I'm nobody."

WHAT HAPPENS WHEN WE RECEIVE OR REJECT GOD'S COMMUNICATION TO US?

Pregnant woman: "I can't afford this baby. I've got no money. I'll have to ask for help. I'll look incompetent. If I don't get help, the baby will starve."

Christian: "I'll look and sound stupid. If no one believes me, not only will I look stupid, I'll probably make God look bad."

The pregnant woman is likely to convince herself that it will be better for the BABY to terminate its life, rather than bring it into a world where it won't receive the best of care.

The Christian reasons that to speak up and share some communication that has just come from the Holy Spirit would bring disgrace on God. The individual might think he would lose credibility as a levelheaded person and a wonderful example of a Christian. He worries that saying words like "God has put it on my heart to tell this congregation that we need to have a period of repentance and fasting and prayer to enable us to receive His instructions," might make others wonder not only about this revelation but also about all the other teachings the individual has ever given.

Pregnant woman: "The rest of my family might suffer if I give birth to this baby."

Christian: "The church may suffer if I share what I'm hearing."

The Christian aborts the thought, the word, the activity. The woman aborts the baby. Both are governed by fear. Just as the woman is kicked and punched from within by the stretching and flexing baby inside of her, so is the Christian prodded and nudged by the Holy Spirit to acknowledge His Presence within.

Abortion of the human baby is an evil thing.

I believe abortion of the Holy Spirit opened the door to physical abortion of babies.

And it doesn't stop there.

Prior to going to the cross, Jesus explained the coming of the Holy Spirit and His purpose. (Before we look at that information, however, it's on my heart to look at why Jesus went to the cross in the first place.

The Apostle Paul explained to the followers of Jesus what the crucifixion did for them:

> *You were dead because of your sins and because your sinful nature was not yet cut away. Then God made you alive with Christ, for he forgave all our sins. He canceled the record of the charges against us and took it away by nailing it to the cross. In this way, he disarmed the spiritual rulers and authorities. He shamed them publicly by his victory over them on the cross* (Colossians 2:13–15).

The cross of Christ. It's the reason Jesus came to Earth. It's why He was willing to be born in that stinky, germ-infested stable. The King of Glory, the Son of God, left Heaven to become human. Mankind needed a way, a path, a means of connecting to God. God didn't rely on man to find the way. God reached out. He made the first move. He always has. He always will.

Jesus knew death was stalking Him. This only-way-arrangement had been the plan between Jesus, God and the Holy Spirit, from the very beginning.

131

"I don't have much more time to talk to you, because the ruler of this world approaches. He has no power over me, but I will do what the Father requires of me, so that the world will know that I love the Father. Come, let's be going" (John 14:30–31).

Now let's return to that time just before Jesus was led away to the cross. He was going to explain an important concept to His followers.

The Role of the Holy Spirit

"But in fact, it is best for you that I go away, because if I don't, the Advocate won't come. If I do go away, then I will send Him to you. And when He comes, he will convict the world of its sin, and of God's righteousness, and of the coming judgment. The world's sin is that it refuses to believe in Me. Righteousness is available because I go to the Father, and you will see Me no more. Judgment will come because the ruler of this world has already been judged.

There is so much more I want to tell you, but you can't bear it now. When the Spirit of Truth comes, He will guide you into all

> *truth. He will not speak on his own but will tell you what he has heard. He will tell you about the future. He will bring me glory by telling you whatever he receives from me. All that belongs to the Father is mine; this is why I said, 'The Spirit will tell you whatever he receives from me'*"(John 16:7–15).

Look at what Jesus said the Holy Spirit would do:

- He would come (HAS COME!!)

- Convince the world of its sin

- Convince the world of God's righteousness

- Convince the world of the coming judgment

- Guide the followers of Jesus into all truth

- Tell the followers of Jesus what He has heard

- Tell the followers of Jesus about the future

- Bring Jesus glory by revealing to the followers of Jesus whatever He receives from Jesus.

Oh reader! Do we see how the Holy Spirit is to affect not only the church but also to affect the world through the church?? Who is to be guided into all truth?

The followers of Jesus! HIS CHURCH!! What do scriptures teach is truth? Jesus said:

> *I am the way, the truth and the life!* (John 14:6).

We also read:

> *The very essence of your words is truth; all your just regulations will stand forever.* (Psalms 119:160, NLT, 2007 edition).

> *All scripture is inspired by God and is useful to teach us what is true and to make us realize what is wrong in our lives. It straightens us out and teaches us to do what is right. It is God's way of preparing us in every way, fully equipped for every good thing God wants us to do* (2 Timothy 3:16–17).

We are to be pointing people to Jesus and to His Word, the Bible. Then, as people encounter Jesus and are introduced to His written Word, the Bible, the Holy Spirit instructs, convicts, and convinces.

Perhaps, if, when we share Jesus with people, we don't stop there, but we also extend God's Presence through spiritual tools like prayers or sharing Bible verses, words of knowledge, or prophecy, with which the Holy Spirit has equipped us, our fellow man would be more inclined to listen to this all-knowing, all-seeing, all-powerful God of ours. I have shared how a timely "word of knowledge" to me changed my view of myself and, indeed, my view of Jesus. Perhaps the Holy Spirit will encourage you to pray a bold prayer for healing over a friend or a complete stranger. Maybe the Holy Spirit will suggest you give a word of prophecy to a friend or neighbor. Unless our culture learns to value God, His teachings from the Bible, and the behavior of those who claim to follow Him, how can we expect people we share with to follow those same teachings? How can they value the Word of God and movement of His Spirit unless they know about Him and His Spiritual interactions? I'm talking about The COMMUNICATION of His Spirit!! Are we telling them??

The work of the Holy Spirit is to convince the world of its sin. That's His job. Well, one of them, anyway. If it's me who is having a haughty attitude or pride or laziness or a judgmental attitude, or any of a zillion other possible bad thoughts or attitudes, it's the JOB of the Holy Spirit to convince me (gently but firmly) that I've messed up and that I seriously need to change. It's what He does. Well, that AND He reminds me that I'm crazy loved by the King of Kings. He tells me of God's goodness and kindness and lets me know that NOTHING can come between me and the Father's love for me!!

> *And I am convinced that nothing can ever separate us from God's love. Neither death nor life, neither angels nor demons, neither our fears for today nor our worries about tomorrow—not even the powers of hell can separate us from God's love. No power in the sky above or in the earth below—indeed, nothing in all creation will ever be able to separate us from the love of God that is revealed in Christ Jesus our LORD* (The Apostle Paul, Romans 8:38–39).

WHAT HAPPENS WHEN WE RECEIVE OR REJECT GOD'S COMMUNICATION TO US?

I'm sure the majority of Christians seriously want to honor God. Yet, as I look around and listen to the concerns of my brothers and sisters in Jesus, I see (and hear) that by and large we do not observe our culture honoring God or His Word! We hear His name taken in vain on TV, in the movies, and in the grocery store. We hear of people clamoring for the death of innocent babies and newborns, equating those deaths with the rights of the parents. Yet God is the very giver of life! We pray for our Lord to DO SOMETHING to change the thinking and behavior of the people on this planet.

What did Jesus tell His followers the Holy Spirit would do? Jesus says HIS SPIRIT is the ONE who is supposed to guide us into ALL TRUTH! Those who put the written Word, (Bible) or thought communication from God/Jesus/Holy Spirit into a box and say, "this can no longer apply to these times and my life" or "this doesn't happen" have, to my thinking, little to no understanding of God's power. If we want to know how to "fix" ourselves and our world, we must first humble ourselves, speak to Him (by praying), read the word of God and follow its teachings, ask Him for forgiveness, and allow Him to direct us.

However, if, instead of looking at the Word of God for direction, if we choose to look at the teachings of men, we may find ourselves in direct opposition to God.

> *Don't copy the behavior and customs of this world, but let God transform you into a new person by changing the way you think. Then you will learn to know God's will for you, which is good and pleasing and perfect* (Romans 12:2).

Like I said before: To find ourselves pushing away from or resisting the Word of God and preferring the words of men, is a very dangerous place to be.

> *All Scripture is inspired by God and is useful to teach us what is true and to make us realize what is wrong in our lives. It corrects us when we are wrong and teaches us to do what is right. God uses it to prepare and*

equip his people to do every good work (2 Timothy 3:16–17).

To start down a slope of resisting what's written in Holy Scripture is to slip onto a path of resisting the ONE who inspired the Bible: God/Jesus/Holy Spirit. I believe the temptation then is to announce: "I'll accept some of your teachings, but not all."

Contrast that attitude to the attitude of Jesus. He didn't hold onto His right, as CREATOR OF THE UNIVERSE, to force mankind to believe in or honor Him. It's a choice. He came as a baby with nothing. No one even wanted to give Him a room in which to be born. So, He went to the barn. He spent His life being kind and healing people. He honored His Father, God, and declared:

"Heaven and earth will disappear, but my words will never disappear" (Matthew 24:35).

"My words?" Did He mean the words He spoke that were recorded in the New Testament? No. John, the Apostle, explained:

> *In the beginning the Word already existed. The Word was with God, and the Word was God. He existed in the beginning with God. God created everything through him, and nothing was created except through him. The Word gave life to everything that was created, and his life brought light to everyone. The light shines in the darkness, and the darkness can never extinguish it.*
>
> *He came into the very world he created, but the world didn't recognize him. He came to his own people, and even they rejected him. But to all who believed him and accepted him, he gave the right to become children of God. They are reborn—not with a physical birth resulting from human passion or plan, but a birth that comes from God* (John 1:1–5, 10–13).

John is helping us to understand that not only was Jesus One with God as God spoke the universe into existence but also as God spoke to Moses and the prophets, communicating truths for them to speak and write, JESUS was that spoken and then written Word. So, when Jesus says HIS words will remain forever, He's talking about HIS Words for direction of mankind. The "things" He created, like this planet and its wonderful everything, WILL go away one day. BUT His Words won't. There it is.

So, to put a book of someone's opinion—about anything—on the same or even a higher level than the Word of the Creator of the universe and His teachings, strikes me as extremely unwise.

One more touching matter to me. Note Jesus' description of the activity of the Holy Spirit. He was there, too. At the beginning. The three of them. Participating as One. We've read much of what Jesus said about Him. Let's also look at what the Apostle Paul said.

> **And we have received God's Spirit (not the world's spirit), so we can know the wonderful things God has freely given us** (1 Corinthians 2:12).

If the Holy Spirit is the Spirt of God, and Jesus and God are One, then the Holy Spirit is part of that wonderful ONENESS!! And now let me remind us of what Jesus said the Holy Spirit would do:

> *"When the Spirit of truth comes, he will guide you into all truth. He will not speak on his own but will tell you what he has heard. He will tell you about the future. He will bring me glory by telling you whatever he receives from me"* (John 16:13–14).

HE WILL NOT PRESENT HIS OWN IDEAS. HE will be telling you what HE has heard. Talk about humility!! He brings glory to Jesus!!

This idea of humility within what we might call the "Godhead," that is God the Father, Jesus—the Son, and the Holy Spirit, is nearly inconceivable. It's beyond any earthly thinking any of us has ever known.

Total power. Total ability. Total control. Total Love. Total humility.

That's the total opposite way of thinking of everyone I know—including me.

The Apostle Paul writes:

> *You must have the same attitude that Christ Jesus had. Though he was God, he did not think of equality with God as something to cling to. Instead, he gave up his divine privileges; he took the humble position of a slave and was born as a human being. When he appeared in human form, he humbled himself in obedience to God and died a criminal's death on a cross. Therefore, God elevated him to the place of highest honor and gave him the name above all other names, that at the name of Jesus every knee should bow, in heaven and on earth and under the earth, and every tongue declare that Jesus Christ is LORD, to the glory of God the Father* (Philippians 2:5–11).

So, our Father has made a way for us. He allowed His Son—who was with Him from the beginning—to come to Earth and pay the penalty for all the bad stuff you or I will ever do. He leaves His Spirit on Earth to communicate with our spirits—inside us! Our job is to listen. Our job is to obey. Our job is to let go of our stubborn pride and follow the example of God, Jesus, and the Holy Spirit. The three-in-ONE, Who planned, from the beginning, to take on the flesh He had created, and die for mankind. A sinless sacrifice. It was the only way. Total humility. Now the Holy Spirit lives on planet Earth and He doesn't call attention to Himself. He serves. He glorifies Jesus. *God forgive me. I have often aborted the nudges of your Holy Spirit.*

The reason I am writing this is that not only do I want to stop aborting but also I want to encourage my brothers and sisters to at least consider the possibility that they may have been aborting Him as well. We must stop quenching Him. We must stop being afraid of allowing Him to give birth to new ways of doing things, new ideas, new songs, and new interactions with others. These new "things"—whatever they are—may not look or feel like what we've been accustomed to, but they will be rooted in love, for God is love (1 John 4:8). Whatever comes from Him will be pure and gentle and willing to yield to others because His word says it will be (James 3:17). Whatever He communicates directly to

His people will be compatible with His Holy written Word. The written Word and the Holy Spirit do not war against each other. They war against the powers of darkness in heavenly places. They war against fear and lust and jealousy and pride and hatred and deceit. Fear has no right to shelter within the Christian body. Fear can be rebuked and ordered to leave by the authority of the name of Jesus, and it must obey.

The Apostle Paul explained:

> *The sinful nature wants to do evil, which is just the opposite of what the Spirit wants. And the Spirit gives us desires that are the opposite of what the sinful nature desires. These two forces are constantly fighting each other, so you are not free to carry out your good intentions.*
>
> *When you follow the desires of your sinful nature, the results are very clear: sexual immorality, impurity, lustful pleasures, idolatry, sorcery, hostility, quarreling, jealousy, outbursts of anger, selfish ambition, dissension, division, envy, drunkenness, wild parties, and other sins like these. Let me tell you again, as I have*

before, that anyone living that sort of life will not inherit the Kingdom of God. But the Holy Spirit produces this kind of fruit in our lives: love, joy, peace, patience, kindness, goodness, faithfulness, gentleness, and self-control. There is no law against these things! Those who belong to Christ Jesus have nailed the passions and desires of their sinful nature to his cross and crucified them there. Since we are living by the Spirit, let us follow the Spirit's leading in every part of our lives. Let us not become conceited, or provoke one another, or be jealous of one another (Galatians 5:17, 19–23A, 24–26).

A Closer Look at Fear—The Path to Pride

In my own life, I've needed to take a close look at pride. My pride. What's behind, or at the root of it? I've come to the conclusion that it's fear. In the scripture shared above, Paul cautions the followers of Jesus to "not become conceited…" In other words, "don't be prideful." Obviously, pride is one that trips up many of us.

But, how does pride find a path into our hearts so often, and, at least with me, so easily?

WHAT HAPPENS WHEN WE RECEIVE OR REJECT GOD'S COMMUNICATION TO US?

Once again, with me, I'm convinced it's fear: fear of being less. Maybe it's the fear of not being all I can or should be, or having less, or being perceived as less, or knowing less. Wait. Less than what? Less than who? That sounds like jealousy.

Bells started going off in my head as I wrote the above, and I couldn't help but think of the story of creation. "In the beginning..." Regardless as to whether or not you view the story of creation as literal, the information God provided Moses to write down concerning the fall of Adam and Eve reveals the very point I'm trying to make.

As you may recall in Genesis 1, 2, and 3, God had created the first man, Adam, after He created all the celestial bodies, including the Earth. After making Adam, God planted a garden: The Garden of Eden. God then placed Adam in the garden and told Adam that he was welcome to eat of any and all fruit in the garden with the exception of the fruit from the Tree of

Knowledge of Good and Evil. God told Adam if he ate of the fruit of that tree, he, Adam, would die.

God then made Eve. Evidently Adam told Eve about the fruit from the Tree of Knowledge of Good and Evil and emphasized that they'd been forbidden to eat it.

Enter Satan. Enemy of God. Enemy of mankind.

Satan asked Eve if God actually told her that neither she nor Adam could eat any of the fruit in the garden. She correctly told Satan that they were allowed to eat any of the fruit—just not the fruit from the Tree of the Knowledge of Good and Evil—or they would die. From the time they were created until this conversation, there is no indication that death in any form had entered the world.

Satan knew Eve may not have understood death fully, and so he lied and proclaimed to her: "You won't die! God knows that your eyes will be opened when you eat it. You will become just like God, knowing everything, both good and evil."

148

WHAT HAPPENS WHEN WE RECEIVE OR REJECT GOD'S COMMUNICATION TO US?

CAUTIONARY NOTE TO US! Whenever we read the Word of God and Satan or a friend, teacher, book or anyone says to us, "No! It doesn't mean what it says," alarms should start going off in our brains. That was EXACTLY Satan's tactic with Eve! Here's the thing...Eve is dead. She did die. Satan lied. He cannot be trusted. God's Word is true. He is honest.

Here's the point: Satan's appeal to Eve was through her pride. What was Satan's implication? "You are less. God knows something you don't. If you eat the fruit, you'll know everything—JUST LIKE HIM!!"

Furthermore, Satan had begun his temptation with the assurance that there would be ZERO adverse consequences: YOU WON'T DIE!!

Adam initially had what I will call a "healthy fear" or, more accurately, *respect* for God and His Word when he, Adam, was instructed to avoid eating from the Tree of the Knowledge of Good and Evil. Why? Because God had told him that DEATH would be the result.

Well, we know what happened. Eve ate and she encouraged Adam to eat and the "eyes" of both of them were opened. They realized they'd sinned. They realized they had disobeyed. They had knowledge of evil. Then they became afraid of how God might react to their disobedience and they hid from him. They were consumed by fear. Life went on but, eventually, they discovered Satan had lied. They did die. God had told them the truth.

Satan had deceived them. There actually were consequences. They didn't have the close unhindered walk with God they'd had every day of their existence up until then. They were experiencing spiritual separation from God for the first time. They were removed from the beautiful garden. They could no longer eat from The Tree of Life. Their bodies were no longer immortal. Hardships came. On and on it went...sorrows and suffering and disease...

How had their downfall—in fact, the downfall of the entire planet—come about? Pride. That whisper from Satan that they could be MORE than they were. Satan's words suggested that God was holding out on them!! He was keeping them at a level LESS than they needed to be.

And, that continues to be his, Satan's, tactics with us even today. How many drug addicts get cleaned up, only to hear, "You know you want more—just one more time. Nothing will come of it—there won't be any consequences." Only something DOES come. Sometimes death. Sometimes the renewal of the full-blown addiction. What does Satan say to the sex addict, the porn addict? "How is anyone going to find out? No one will know. No consequences." Except that there are consequences. In fact, I'm convinced that it's generally Satan, himself, who makes SURE there are consequences for his victims. He hates us. Look how the Apostle Peter explained Satan's antics:

Stay alert! Watch out for your great enemy, the devil. He prowls around like a roaring lion, looking for someone to devour. Stand firm against him, and be strong in your faith. Remember that your family of believers all over the world is going through the same kind of suffering you are (1 Peter 5:8,9).

Furthermore, in the book of Revelation, written by the Apostle John, we read how Satan spends all his time, all day, every day:

"...the accuser of our brothers and sisters has been thrown down to earth—the one who <u>accuses them before</u> <u>our God day and</u> <u>night"</u> (Revelation 12:10B, words are underlined by the author for emphasis).

I know you recall the teaching about how the Spirit of God lives inside of us and we get to know something of the mind of Christ. I'm convinced that all that accusing that goes on before the throne of our God—against us—is largely heard by us! As we discussed earlier in the book, we have the mind of Christ! If we're "in his mind," it's understandable that we'd hear much of what He hears. So, look at what happens: Satan searches the Earth for someone "to devour." Then, no sooner does he spring the trap, devouring us in something evil, but he starts announcing to God, "LOOK WHAT MARY JUST DID (or said or thought or...) MARY IS A HYPOCRITE! MARY is a PHONEY!!!" I hear it! AND I know there is at least some truth to what he's saying, so I feel lousy.

HOWEVER.

Wait a minute. There's a better comeback:

BUT JESUS!!

YES! Hallelujah!! Jesus went to the cross, DIED for ME, Mary the PHONEY! Mary the HYPOCRITE! And now, because Jesus CAME BACK TO LIFE, I live a NEW LIFE every day in HIM!! I'm FORGIVEN!! Jesus forgives and sets me free as many times as I sin!! HALLELUJAH!! Thank you, JESUS!!

And where did this faulty thinking start? Something having to do with pride—rooted in fear.

Make no mistake—fear has personality. It is not simply an abstract concept. It has personality and intent.

A number of years ago as I looked more closely at the biblical story of Cain's jealousy of Abel (Genesis 4), God pointed out something to me that I had missed earlier. At one point, after God had been displeased with Cain's offering, but pleased with Abel's, God went to Cain and had a little talk with him. God told Cain that He could see into his heart. He knew that Cain was struggling with jealousy toward Abel. God warned Cain that sin was **crouching** at his door and **wanting to devour** him. The old King James version refers to sin as "he" and God encouraged Cain that he (Cain) must rule over "him"—sin. The newer translations refer to sin as "it." I asked a Hebrew scholar if the original Hebrew actually said "he" or "it." I was told that the word used in that case could be translated either "he" or "it." In any event, the picture of sin "crouching at the door" as if waiting to attack and wanting to "devour" Cain certainly suggests personality with intent.

WHAT HAPPENS WHEN WE RECEIVE OR REJECT GOD'S COMMUNICATION TO US?

My reason for pointing out the personality of evil is to suggest that not only have we, in Christendom, been guilty, in my opinion, of widespread rejection of the Holy Spirit, but also we have been guilty of failing to realize that we have an adversary with personality and intent. In fact, it is probably this failure to recognize the enemy that keeps us from taking up our holy weapons of warfare to defend ourselves and defeat him.

If people don't realize they are in battle, they won't carry a sword. When people are ignorant of the ramifications of germs, they fail to wash their hands. It is amazing to think that it was only in the mid-1800s when doctors discovered they needed to wash their hands to remove germs between examinations of sick and well patients! (Google the name Semmelweis.) Before Semmelweis, doctors hadn't yet recognized the "enemy"!! (AND even then, a large portion of the medical community refused to believe and scoffed at those who proposed such a practice!)

Now give those germs personality! (This practice, to my knowledge, is fictitious!) It's one thing to think, *Oh nuts, I've got a bug, I need to take some medicine.* It feels totally different to think, *It found me!! It's working its way through my body WANTING to make me sick!!* We don't think of germs as having personality. A germ is an it. It doesn't think, it doesn't plan, it just exists and sometimes when we get too many of the wrong kind they make us sick. There's nothing personal. It just happens.

If I merely think of my spiritual enemy as an "it," I am likely to think of "it" as being a concept, which I can easily control with my thinking. If I am experiencing jealousy, I may think to myself, *This jealousy is groundless. That person has weaknesses too* or *He received the award this year, but perhaps I will receive it next year. In the meantime, I will decide to be happy for him.* We can thereby make a mental decision to deal with our jealousy with logic and reason. The problem comes when we realize that our jealousy hasn't gone away even with all of our mental gymnastics. The problem is that

attitudes like jealousy, hatred, and selfishness are part
of what scriptures refer to as our "sinful nature." This
sinful nature has "desires" that are in conflict with the
Holy Spirit. From the Apostle Paul:

> *So I say, let the Holy Spirit guide your lives.
> Then you won't be doing what your sinful
> nature craves. The sinful nature wants to do
> evil, which is just the opposite of what the
> Spirit wants. And the Spirit gives us desires
> that are the opposite of what the sinful
> nature desires. These two forces are
> constantly fighting each other, so you are not
> free to carry out your good intentions*
> (Galatians 5:16–17).

Why would the Holy Spirit be in conflict with an
"it"? The conflict is because of the intent of "sinful
nature" to destroy us. Think of it: Jealousy does me
absolutely no good. It makes me miserable. Hatred and
selfishness don't cause me to smile at the world either.
Those emotions are part of an arsenal of the enemy of
the Holy Spirit/God/Jesus. Who is that enemy? The

devil. This arsenal of weapons is aided by the personality of the user—the devil—and his weapons.

Think about this fact: Whenever we are dealing with jealousy, we hear a constant barrage in our brains of how unfair life is!! *How come I didn't find that dress first?? How come I didn't have the money for that car or that trip or whatever? Why didn't anyone say how nice I looked when I walked into the room?? Why does everyone like him?? I'm MUCH more intelligent than he could ever hope to be!!* The comments go on and on and on and IF WE LISTEN we only become more miserable. We're convinced all those comments are right! They're justified!! BUT we are miserable. Actually, jealousy is supposed to make you miserable. It's a tool of Satan. He doesn't like mankind. He doesn't like you. He wants you to be stuck in fear.

Quick Reminder of the Power of our Lord

Contrast all the negative emotions with the Holy Spirit who produces fruit at the other end of the spectrum. Let's hear, again, from Apostle Paul:

> *But when the Holy Spirit controls our lives, He will produce this kind of fruit in us: love, joy, peace, patience, kindness, goodness, faithfulness, gentleness, and self-control. Here there is no conflict with the law. Those who belong to Christ Jesus have nailed the passions and desires of their sinful nature to His cross and crucified them there. If we are living now by the Holy Spirit, let us follow the Holy Spirit's leading in every part of our lives. Let us not become conceited, or irritate one another, or be jealous of one another* (Galatians 5:22–26).

That's the kind of stuff to cuddle up with at night. You can't help but smile just saying the words. The Holy Spirit—Who IS positive, loving, has a radiant personality, and is constantly in conflict with "sinful nature," doesn't want us to be miserable. He doesn't want us to hurt. That doesn't mean He won't allow someone else to get promoted over us, or someone else to receive the praises of men instead of us. He will, however, give us a way to deal with whatever frustrations come to us. By various means—through prayer, through the power of the love Jesus showed for us by going to the cross, and by His decision to stay UP on that cross when He could have come down—we have the means to release from jealousy and bitterness and anger. All those feelings just dissipate. Breaking up those emotions inside of us is just part of the activity of the Holy Spirit.

In addition to giving us the gifts of "fruits of the Spirit," that help us with living, the Holy Spirit also reveals truth to us when we are in the thick of the mental battle. *What's really going on here?*, we wonder as our emotions are all torn up inside.

Back to the Brutal Battle with Fear

A number of years ago, I was in a deep, difficult battle with my emotions. I became aware of a pervasive sadness that seemed to be a part of my every day. It stayed with me from the time I woke up in the morning until I went to bed at night. At first, I thought it was simply some form of hormonal fluke. It would pass. It always did. But, the days and weeks wore on, and the sadness stayed. I would find myself washing dishes, and I would just burst out crying. Repeatedly, I would think to myself: *Get a grip! Don't let the family see you like this!* At times I wondered if God was allowing me to experience the sadness of the entire world. This sadness had a depth to it that was miserable, dark, and almost terrifying.

I thought of going to see a counselor. I thought of what I would say when we met.

Me: "I'm sad."

Counselor: "What's wrong?"

Me: "I haven't a clue.

Counselor: "How's your marriage?"

Me: "It's not perfect, but it's pretty good."

Counselor: "How's your relationship with your children?"

Me: "I'm not a perfect mom, but we all get along alright."

We would end up sitting and staring at each other. I didn't have anything to "pin" it on. I was just sad—EXTREMELY, HORRIBLY sad.

One morning I awoke, and for the briefest moment, I felt fine. No sorrow, no darkness, nothing. I yawned and smiled—not even aware that I felt one way or another—when suddenly, BOOM! Almost like a blow to my abdomen, the sadness raced in. I doubled up in pain and spoke to it: "Ha! Ha! You were late today! I had two glorious seconds of relief!"

Clarity in the Battle

Later that day, I went to the grocery store and had to force myself to walk up and down the aisles putting canned goods into the basket. What I wanted to do was to run screaming from the store. The sadness was trying desperately hard to totally take me over. Yet, I was aware—wonderfully aware—that there was something inside of me that held the sadness at bay. Something seemed to say to that evil that wanted to overwhelm me, "You may come this far but no farther." After I paid for my groceries and was walking through the parking lot, I started praying inside my head:

Lord, what IS this sadness? What in the world is happening to me?

An inaudible thought replied, *What does it feel like?*

Internally, I answered: *It feels invasive. It was outside of me this morning and then it came inside.*

The thought then asked, *What invades the body?*

Germs invade the body, I answered.

Is this a germ?"

No! This isn't a germ. Germs don't have personality. This has personality.

Once again the questioning continued in my head. *What has personality and invades the body?*

Hesitantly, I answered. *A spirit can enter the body and a spirit has personality.*

The probing continued, *Is this My spirit? Is this Spirit Holy?*

Without hesitating I inwardly shouted, *NO!!*

Then, once more, I was asked, *What kind of a spirit enters the body, has personality, and is not holy?"*

My mind was racing, trying to grasp the truth that was gradually dawning on me. *A demon. A demon can enter the body, has personality and is evil.*

How can one get rid of a demon?

There is no way, other than by casting it out in the name of Jesus.

Then do it.

Standing right there, at the back of my car in the parking lot of the super market, I prayed out loud a simple prayer that parted the darkness and purchased my freedom:

> By the power of the name of Jesus, I rebuke you. You have no power over me. I have been bought

with the blood of Jesus. I am His child. By the authority of the name of Jesus Christ, Who was and is and always will be, come out of me!

And that was it. I heard no screams, no drums, no electricity shot out of my body. Nothing. Only peace. Only sweet joy and happiness and a sense that I had been cleansed.

Until the next day. The next morning I woke up just fine. No sadness, no hint of what had been plaguing me for the past several weeks. Then, I had a brief, very brief mental struggle—doubt, suspicion, about my teenage daughter, and her conduct. WHAM!! At the instant I had entertained the thought, the sadness invaded again. Immediately, I realized the fallacy of the doubt about my daughter and renounced it. I then called on the authority of the name of Jesus to rid me from this menace once again. However, THIS time, in addition to being rid of the demon, I also received, inside my head, the information: *He thought he was welcome because you were having bad thoughts about your daughter!*

REVELATION!! My bad thoughts (doubts about my daughter's conduct) put out a welcome mat to a demon!! One thought!! One almost insignificant little thought caused a demon from hell to enter my body and make me miserable!! The Holy Spirit not only delivered me from his grasp but also educated me as to the why of the grasp in the first place. I had been given a spiritual tool—a wonderful, cleansing, life-changing spiritual tool. The name of Jesus is powerful. There is nothing more powerful than Jesus in Heaven or on Earth, BUT if I hadn't used that tool, I might still be plagued by that demon!

Sometime after that, in Sunday morning Bible class, I shared this story. I forget the exact topic or text we were studying, but I thought it was an appropriate and important time to share my experience. After I told the story, the teacher simply said "thank you, Mary," and that was that—until after class.

After class an older, very dignified sister approached me and thanked me for speaking up and sharing my experience. "I had a similar one many years ago, but I've never told anyone because I thought they'd think I was nuts!" I asked her to tell me her story. She did, and it involved a visual manifestation of a demon witnessed by herself and another person until she rebuked it/him in the name of Jesus! Her story could have encouraged countless others, but this precious sister aborted telling the incident because of her fear of sharing and "sounding nuts."

Christians must become aware that ours is not a battle of words, of theology, or of translations. The battle belongs to the Lord. He has fought and won. We are to use the tools He has prepared for us. The battle we fight is refusal to believe that we are, first and foremost, spiritual beings. If we fail to allow the Holy Spirit to do His mighty works within and through us, we quench and abort him and abet our enemy—the very one who wants to destroy us! If we fail to realize that we HAVE an enemy, then we fail to pick up our tools and use them!!

One more note about sharing my story of deliverance from a demon: At one point, when I was relaying my experience to a couple who had also been brought up in the cessationist tradition, the husband listened but then said something to the effect of "Yes, Mary, but what we read in scripture is that it was only Jesus or the Apostles who were able to cast out demons." I simply reminded him that Jesus said that those of us who believe in Him would be able to do the same and even "greater works" than what He'd done. I hope that doesn't come across as haughty. I only know that I'd been tormented, and because of the power of THE NAME of JESUS and HIS power within me, by invoking HIS name, my tormentor had been removed!! PRAISE YOU, JESUS!!

> *"I tell you the truth, anyone who believes in me will do the same works I have done, and even greater works, because I am going to be with the Father. You can ask for anything in my name, and I will do it, so that the Son*

can bring glory to the Father" (John 14:12–
13).

Please also note that I had never heard a sermon,
nor to my memory, have I ever read a book about a
person having the ability to cast out a demon from
within one's own body! The knowledge that I was being
attacked by a demonic presence had come, I believe,
through the Holy Spirit Himself!! THANK YOU,
JESUS!! HE is the Teacher! HE was/is my counselor,
my personal trainer. He had put people in place all my
life who had encouraged me to read and become
familiar with His Word, the Bible. Recalling the
scriptures I'd read, and applying them to my situation
by the encouragement of His Holy Spirit, was what led
me out of spiritual bondage and into spiritual Freedom
in Jesus!! HALLELUJAH!

National-Sized Attacks and Spiritual Battles
Since those in my circle of worship hadn't been taught
about a supernatural downloading of information via

the Holy Spirit, is it any wonder that when the enemy decided to brazenly launch an attack on major cities of the United States, ("one nation under God"), and at least one in my fellowship had been warned, that she had absolutely no idea where the warning had come from nor what she was supposed to do with it? Here's what happened to the U.S., and what happened with my friend. As I write now, it's 2020; In the following section, I'm reflecting back on the following memories…

Today is Friday, September 14, 2001. On Tuesday, September 11, 2001, terrorists hijacked four U.S. commercial jets and crashed three of them into heavily occupied buildings. The fourth crashed into an open field in Pennsylvania. Over and over, the U.S. citizens are asking, "How could this have happened?" The answer? We weren't prepared because terrorism wasn't seen as a real threat on American soil. Security was breached at the airports probably because those in charge of security hadn't been trained to look for the types of weapons the hijackers used. Or, the security agents may simply have been careless, not paying attention at the right times. They may have been unconcerned about what they saw. They could not imagine that anyone would do what the hijackers did.

The fourth plane, however, did not hit its intended target. At the moment, the thinking is that some of the passengers on the fourth plane, after making cell phone calls to loved ones came to realize the intent of the hijackers. These passengers quickly realized the battle they were in and decided to use the tools they had— themselves—available to stop their enemies. One passenger, talking on his cell phone to his wife and learning of the plane crashes into the World Trade Center and the Pentagon, told her "we're going to do something." The flight recorder seems to have picked up sounds of a scuffle in the cockpit of that plane and someone shouting "GET OUT OF HERE!!" Shortly afterwards, the plane crashed into the open field. All passengers died. Once the men knew the intent of their enemy, they were **willing** to wage "war" against the hijackers and keep the plane from killing more innocent people. They willed to fight. Their knowledge of the intent of their enemy prompted them to do something.

If you could recognize yourself as a spiritual being with spiritual forces surrounding you—some wanting to destroy you, some wanting to aid you, would you want to know:

1. How to discern the good from the bad, and

2. Once identified, how to defeat the bad?

The world is reeling under the influence of Satan and his demons. However, if Christians pray and seek guidance from the Holy Spirit, He will tell us how He wants this battle fought. He will reveal to us what it is we're doing wrong and how He wants us to behave. But first, we must learn to listen. We must pray and then we must be silent. "BE SILENT" He says, "And KNOW I AM GOD!" (Psalms 46:10). He is the General. He is the King of Kings and the Lord of Lords. Let's await HIS battle plans instead of constantly rushing in with our own. Too many of our people have been wounded by carrying out plans that were never ordained nor blessed by our Commander in Chief. Let us pray, then let us listen. Then let us pray some more, and only then should we act. But act we must!!

Today's date is now Thursday, September 20, 2001. Last night I went with my family to our weekly Bible study at our congregation. When I was there, a dear sister-in-Christ, in agonized tears, told me of a vision the Lord had given to her on the morning of September 11, 2001—Terror Tuesday.

This precious sister shared with me that she had been a guest in a friend's home out of state on that dreadful morning. She said she had been in bed, praying, when she suddenly had a vision of two airplanes crashing into the twin towers of the World Trade Center. She also saw a plane crash into the Pentagon. She then heard the words: "Call the Pentagon" and "call your son." At the time, she had a son in New York City. The time was 5:40 a.m. EST.

Her reaction? She slapped herself in the face and told herself "snap out of it! You're going crazy!!" She did not call the Pentagon. She did not call her son, but she did continue to pray. Later that morning she and her friend received a call from the woman's husband to turn on the television: the Twin Towers of the World Trade Center had been attacked by airplanes. Horrified, she desperately tried to call her son. And then the Pentagon was hit. Eventually she and her son connected, and she learned that he had run for seven blocks to escape the falling debris and smoke, but that he was fine. She, however, was not.

"It's my fault, Mary! It's my fault! He (God) SHOWED me what was going to happen! He TOLD me to call the Pentagon, and I didn't do it!!" This woman's guilt is tremendous. We prayed and I reminded her that the whole reason Jesus went to the cross was to forgive us of our sins, so that guilt and fear of God and His displeasure would not consume us. Intellectually, she knows that, but emotionally, knowing of the thousands of people who died, this precious sister is holding herself responsible. She's wrong to do so, and I've prayed that God will awaken her to His mercy for her—but right now, she's hurting.

How many others, I wonder, were given similar visions? How many others dismissed any word of knowledge or vision as simply a wayward thought or a sign of their mental/emotional demise? How ironic that we Christians, the very people who pray continuously for peace and God's favor on our country, would be afraid of sharing information from Him on ways to protect the citizenry! And the reason we don't share the information?

1. We haven't learned to recognize His communications as being from God/Jesus/Holy Spirit and/or

2. We're afraid of ridicule.

God help us.

Father, please help us TRUST in YOU and YOUR WORD to fight fear, personal spiritual battles, and even worldwide spiritual battles with the power, confidence, and tools YOU have given us. THANK YOU, HOLY SPIRIT, for living in us and communicating Your power to and through us!!

Chapter Four

COMMUNICATION FROM GOD—
"OKAY, LORD. MAKE ME
READY TO RECEIVE!"

Moving Past Failure

As I sat with my previously mentioned sister-in-Christ and listened to her agonize over her missed opportunity to "do something," (after she had a vision of the terror to come on September 11, also known as Terror Tuesday), I kept thinking two things:

1. I wished there had been better training within the church to help our members learn to recognize the nudges or sometimes the voice or even visions of God—that come to us through the Holy Spirit—and

2. I thought of my own missed opportunities.

What do you do when it becomes clear that God has communicated to you, has given you an assignment, and you didn't do it? To whom do you go when The Comforter of the universe is the one you've offended—when you quench the Holy Spirit? In Scripture, God's command is as clear as it can be: *"Do not quench the Holy Spirit"* (1 Thessalonians 5:19, NIV). Nonetheless, it's common practice, I believe, within the church to do just that. So, What do we do when we've failed?

We know what to do when we sin, as Christians, right?

So, perhaps it might help to look at the relationship between sinning and quenching the Spirit. According to Merriam Webster, sin is a transgression of the law of God.[4] In other words, it is failing to do what God says to do or doing what God said not to do. Since Paul, via guidance by the Holy Spirit, wrote in the book of 1 Thessalonians 5:19 (NLT), *"Do not quench the Holy Spirit,"* then, when we do stifle His nudges, His whispers, His visions by saying "no" or dismissing them as silly or illogical or, for whatever reason, then yes, I believe that when we quench the flow of the Spirit, we have sinned. Since Timothy taught in 2 Timothy 3:16 that **all scripture is inspired by God,** then what Paul wrote about not quenching the Spirit had to have come from God. So, what do we do when we stifle or quench His activity through us?

What do we teach our children to do when they've done wrong? We teach them to apologize. Likewise, if we're willing to take responsibility for our failure, we say we're sorry. The following verse tells us how to be contrite and what to do—admit our brokenness and turn from it:

> *The sacrifice you desire is a broken spirit. You will not reject a broken and repentant heart, O God* (Psalm 51:17).

Matthew 9:6 records Jesus stating that He has the authority on Earth to forgive sins. The apostle Paul quotes Jesus as having told him to go

> (to people everywhere) *'to open their eyes, so they may turn from darkness to light and from the power of Satan to God. Then they will receive forgiveness for their sins and be given a place among God's people, who are set apart by faith in me'* (Acts 26:18, words in parenthesis inserted by the author for clarification.)

Forgiveness of sins is available to all of us who look to God/Jesus for forgiveness. When we miss opportunities to serve, when we refuse to obey, when we quench the Holy Spirit, we need to say we're sorry.

Becoming Aware of His Communication

Or, perhaps you're not aware of having disobeyed an instruction from God. Perhaps you're not aware of ever having heard from God at all except in having a sense of His presence through the written Word. Perhaps you're conscious of your shortcomings in relation to other instructions of Jesus such as loving your neighbor, avoiding lust, avoiding hypocrisy, or resisting a judgmental attitude, etc. If any thinking or behavior that runs contrary to the Word of God has found a "home" in our heart, and if we genuinely want to hear from our Lord, then we've got to be willing to part with those thoughts/behaviors.

The Christian's relationship to God/Jesus/Holy Spirit is one of saved to the Savior, sheep to the Shepherd, child to the Father, beloved to the One who loves. We are also referred to as the vessel in His hands. He does to us as He chooses. Since He is love and He loves us, we can rest assured that whatever He does to us will be out of love, for the purpose of bringing us into a greater awareness of His love for us.

When we Christians are aware of God's great love for us, we need not fear the ways God may choose to communicate His love for us.

Please don't be afraid to open yourself up to ANY FORM of communication from God. Please don't tell others that God no longer communicates directly to His children. Please don't feel left out if you have no awareness of God having communicated directly to you. Although all Christians are promised the indwelling of the Holy Spirit, we are told that He gives special abilities or gifts to each of us BUT that we're not all alike (see 1 Corinthians 12). God may be honing gifts within you that lie dormant in me. The point is, though, that WE MUST NOT TELL ANYONE WHO THINKS HE OR SHE HAS HEARD FROM GOD THAT THEY COULD NOT POSSIBLY HAVE DONE SO!! Likewise, I must never tell you that the gift God is developing or has developed within you is not from Him or is useless or without merit.

We must test all information and informants. Do they, or are they willing to say that "Jesus is Lord"? Paul writes that no one can say "Jesus is Lord" except by the Holy Spirit (1 Corinthians 12:3). If an individual is claiming to have received information from the Holy Spirit, he/she will also be subject to obeying all the teachings of Jesus and acknowledging Jesus as Lord and Savior. When that individual makes mistakes, he, like everyone else, must repent, say he's sorry, and ask for forgiveness.

Do you want to hear from God outside of His written word? Ask Him! Luke 11 records Jesus' words:

> *"So if you sinful people know how to give good gifts to your children, how much more will your heavenly Father give the Holy Spirit to those who ask him"* (Luke 11:13).

Jesus didn't put a time limit nor an age limit on making that request. He also says:

> *"For everyone who asks, receives. Everyone who seeks, finds. And to everyone who knocks, the door will be opened"* (Matthew 7:8).

There is no limit to God's love for each of us. Please do not resist His attempts to reveal Himself to you.

And, as He reveals Himself, TELL OTHERS so that they might learn of Him and give Him the praise He deserves. Let me encourage all leaders within the church to encourage your flock to TELL OTHERS what God is doing in their lives. There's power in the activity of the Holy Spirit. Hearing of that activity convinces and convicts others. Please, let us not keep this good news to ourselves.

Choosing to Receive from and to Communicate with God

Perhaps, at this point, your heart has been touched and you find yourself truly wanting to be more receptive of the Holy Spirit within. You may be asking, "What should I do?" Well, what did Jesus say?

> *"Keep on asking, and you will receive what you ask for. Keep on seeking, and you will find. Keep on knocking, and the door will be opened to you"* (Matthew 7:7).

I believe He'd like you to pray to ask Him how He would like you to proceed.

If you need wisdom, ask our generous God, and he will give it to you. He will not rebuke you for asking (James 1:5).

Is there private sin He wants you to address? Then ask Him to help you deal with it. Do you sense the need to gather with others to pray? Ask Him who to contact and how often He wants you to gather, etc., etc., etc. In short, allow the Holy Spirit to take you by the spiritual hand and guide you. That's what He does!!

If you've paid even partial attention to the various dates I've mentioned along the way, you've become aware that I've been writing these thoughts for years. As I write this section, it is October 10th, 2019. I now live in Tennessee. The Governor of the state of Tennessee is Bill Lee. Governor Lee has proclaimed October 10, 2019, to be a day of Prayer and Fasting*, and has asked all citizens in the state of Tennessee to join him in this observance. In just a couple of hours, my husband and I plan to go downtown (Nashville) to take part in a large praise gathering with my brothers and sisters in Jesus. I'm sure we'll acknowledge to our Lord that we've messed up. We'll apologize for all our ungodly behavior and thank Him for allowing Jesus to take the punishment for each of us. I'll definitely be thanking Jesus for taking my punishment. We'll pray for ourselves and our nation. Then...well, let's just keep our eyes and hearts attuned to our Lord and see how He will respond. After all, He encouraged us to do the very things we are about to do:

> *...if my people who are called by my name will humble themselves and pray and seek my face and turn from their wicked ways, I will hear from heaven and will forgive their sins and restore their land* (2nd Chronicles 7:14).

I was prepared to wrap up my writing at this point, but my Father seems to have had a different idea.

Enter Coronavirus: Learning from a Pandemic

Personally, seeing the entire planet "at war" with an invisible (to the naked eye) enemy (a virus), and the plague of locusts in Africa, and the frequency of earthquakes, I can't help but wonder if the Lord is trying to communicate something to us!!

Sigh. At this moment, in the Spring of 2020, due to the pandemic of the Coronavirus, my husband and I are quarantined in our house in Tennessee. Each of my children, in fact, our whole country, is supposed to be quarantined in their homes as well. Not everyone is complying, but, many of us are. We're weary of NOT being able to go visit family, NOT getting with friends, NOT going to worship with our Christian family, etc., etc., etc. My children are all working from home. My grandchildren are all being homeschooled now. But, we're the ones who are fortunate. Far too many people aren't able to go to work—virtually or in person—and they're suffering economically. Although Congress has just passed a bill to get money into the hands of the majority of the population, huge concerns linger. Will it be enough? Will jobs ever return?? On and on. People are worried. Many are hungry. Many are sick. Many are dying.

What to do? What to do?

I'm thinking of the multitudes of people who are frightened, hungry, and crying out to God. When will this end? What's around the corner? People are angry! Frustrated! They (we!) want answers. Most of all, we want COVID 19 to GO AWAY!!

Here's another troubling matter: the number of cases are growing largely because we, as a people, refuse to believe we truly need to be the ONEs to quarantine. After schools had been closed and we'd been asked to self-quarantine, David and I decided to take a drive through the countryside just to "see the world." On our way back home we drove down a street that was full of strip malls. Over and over we passed parking lots that were full of cars. Clearly, people were not taking the epidemic seriously. (Believe me, my poor husband has nearly had to restrain me to keep me in the house! IT'S HARD!!)

"Surely it won't matter if I get together with MY friends", some seem to say. "Let THEM quarantine. Not me! I'm going to have fun!!"

Except that it's not fun to watch others get sick and die. It's not fun to watch our economy slow down, people lose their jobs, their food, and their homes.

That kind of thinking reminds me of the porn addict who truly believes he or she is only effecting themselves. Or the recovering alcoholic or drug addict who honestly thinks that just one more drink or one more hit won't matter. Or the one who chooses to allow bitterness or anger or hate or righteous indignation to consume their thoughts thinking *how I feel inside doesn't hurt anyone. It doesn't matter.* All of it always matters.

As for me, I was willing to simply hit my knees and pray for the world without addressing, in this book, what's on my heart regarding this virus. I wanted to send the book to my editor and just consider my writing finished. But the Holy Spirit...Look at what has happened: I've been working on a book I've titled *Communication from God*, for a very long time. Our country and, in fact, the world, is experiencing an unprecedented lock down. Since I am one who normally looks for God's presence in just about everything, WHY was I trying to avoid looking into what God might be saying to me/us right now? Is it because the answer might rattle us/me?

I have received no vision nor audible direction from Him regarding COVID 19. Once again, what I felt was more like an inward moaning, or a heaviness of heart when I, at first, opted to say nothing. The following, I believe, is what my Lord Jesus would have me share.

Our society has gradually come to accept, approve, and even celebrate behavior that God forbade throughout scripture such as taking God's name in vain, sex outside of marriage, bribery, homosexuality, pornography, divorce, murder of the unborn, greed, failure to honor God in one day of the week above all others, lying, gossip, verbally assaulting government leaders and each other, arrogance, etc., etc., etc. If we're honest, we can each find certain of our own behaviors incompatible with the Spirit of God. The question is, am I determined to have my own way—thus making whatever it is the idol or "god" I worship—or am I willing to listen to Holy Scripture, from the One Who made me and loves me and calls me to head in a different direction? Society has decided to treat much of our current misguided behavior as being normal, acceptable, or even good. Acceptable to whom?

To many of us, our society looks and acts/reacts to life as though it's sick. I'm thinking particularly of the many, many people who take antidepressants, the many who are addicted to alcohol, porn, drugs, the internet, the many who commit suicide, etc. When any of us gets sick, what do we do? Don't we generally try to take a moment and figure out how we got that way? I usually ask myself, *What did I do to cause this? Did I eat something contaminated? Have I caught a germ? Have I been pushing too hard? Do I need to get some rest? What did I do??*

Beyond the physical, there's also a spiritual component to feeling bad emotionally. Since one of the fruits of the Spirit of God within me is joy, when I'm not experiencing joy, I try to ask myself: *Am I somehow blocking that delicious fruit. Am I harboring an attitude that can lead to my misery? Am I bitter? Resentful? Jealous? Fearful? etc.? If so, am I willing to release those emotions to the power of Jesus, say I'm sorry, ask Him to forgive me, and fill me with Himself?*

Generally, if I am holding onto some form of bitterness or resentment, it's because I honestly think I'm entitled to feel that way. I'm guessing the majority of you reading this can relate to that kind of emotional arms-folding. Yet the result of my stubborn holding on to yucky emotions is that I FEEL MISERABLE!! I feel like I'm JUSTIFIED in feeling bitter or resentful, etc., but my hate, bitterness, whatever, MOSTLY hurts ME!! BUT, whenever I've been able to stop myself—

certainly because the Holy Spirit was involved—a calm of peace and joy somewhat miraculously has filled my inner being. HALLELUJAH!

Conversely, what happens when we refuse to let go of a resentment or any emotion (for which we feel entitled) that blocks our Lord's joy or peace to us? I'm aware that some emotions are based on traumas from childhood that have never been successfully addressed. Sometimes professional help is needed, but always, our Lord is needed. He's the mender of broken hearts and the healer of deep, deep wounds. Or perhaps we're engaged in or have been approving of rebellious activity such as ANYTHING God forbade throughout scripture. Let me remind us of the time, long, long ago when God destroyed the people of the Earth (with the exception of ONE man and his family), with a universal flood. We read in the book of Genesis:

> *The LORD observed the extent of human wickedness on the earth, and he saw that everything they thought or imagined was*

consistently and totally evil. So the LORD was sorry he had ever made them and put them on the earth. It broke his heart. And the LORD said, "I will wipe this human race I have created from the face of the earth. Yes, and I will destroy every living thing—all the people, the large animals, the small animals that scurry along the ground, and even the birds of the sky. I am sorry I ever made them." But Noah found favor with the LORD (Genesis 6:5–8).

WHERE had the Lord been concentrating? ON THEIR THOUGHTS!! It starts in our thoughts then continues into behavior and HE is aware!

Let's recall, too, how the prophet, Isaiah, warned the people of his day. He wrote:

Destruction is certain for those who drag their sins behind them, tied with cords of falsehood (Isaiah 5:18, NLT—1996 edition).

In this verse, dragging their sins behind them with cords of falsehood would be like saying, "Hey everyone! LOOK AT ME! There's nothing wrong with what I'm doing and I plan to do more of it!!"

Isaiah continues:

> *Destruction is certain for those who say that evil is good and good is evil; that dark is light and light is dark; that bitter is sweet and sweet is bitter.*
>
> *Destruction is certain for those who think they are wise and consider themselves to be clever.*
>
> *Destruction is certain for those who are heroes when it comes to drinking, who boast about all the liquor they can hold.*
>
> *They take bribes to pervert justice. They let the wicked go free while punishing the innocent.*
>
> *Therefore, they will disappear like burning straw. Their roots will rot and their flowers wither, for they have rejected the law of the LORD Almighty. They have despised the word of the Holy One of Israel. That is why the anger of the LORD burns against his people. That is why he has raised his fist to crush them* (Isaiah 5:20–25A, NLT—1996 edition).

In other words, there ARE consequences for us spurning the teachings of the Word of God! There ARE consequences for saying that what God said is wrong is not wrong. With Adam and Eve, Satan told Eve she would not die if she ate the forbidden fruit. She ate and she DID die! In the days of Noah, God sent a universal flood. In the days of Isaiah, God sent in waring armies to conquer.

Right now virtually every country on the planet is "at war," flooded by a virus we cannot see. Is this all just happenstance? Or should we be asking ourselves, "Have I contributed to this "plague? Is there anything I can do?" Because a plague is sure what it seems like. When we look at the pictures or read the reports of the simultaneous plague of locusts in Africa, or earthquakes throughout the earth can we honestly, rationally conclude that this is all simply "coincidental" timing?

For those of us who believe in and look to God, this COVID 19 quarantine season is surely a time for self-reflection, penance, and asking our Lord what He'd like us to do. For those who don't believe, it seems to me, this would be a good time to ask if God (in whom you don't believe), is trying to get your attention! Then talk to Him, and ask HIM to communicate to you!!

Our angst in the moment, wariness of the future, and an almost helpless sense of being able to defend against this enemy reminds me of a time in my life when I found myself constantly on the floor, praying, and crying out to God. My life seemed such a joke. I had tried to teach my children about God. I had tried to do right and be right, and it just wasn't working! Two of my teenage children had actually told me they weren't even sure they believed in God anymore. My heart ached. I was so sorry. Obviously I had failed them. Lousy mother. Jesus was THE most important being in the universe to me and I hadn't even been able to help my children connect to Him. I recall sobbing on my knees in their bedroom, totally distressed, begging Him to HELP US!! My heart was broken. I was desperate for Him! I couldn't "fix" my children, and I couldn't fix me. I needed Him to intervene and DO SOMETHING!! I'm not sure if it was that same day or the next, but I was on the floor—again—when I heard Him inside my head. He asked me, *How long will you cry?* Although I'm a very emotional person, I'm also fairly logical. He'd asked a question, so I began to think before I answered. For the briefest moment I wondered if it was a "trick" question. I'd been crying out to Him for years! I intended to cry for as long as it would take! That answer had just formed in my head when He began to ask, *Mary, if I don't "fix"* (the children) *in five years, will you continue to cry?*

Now, I'd been crying on the floor, nearly daily, for a couple of years. I quickly reasoned, sure! If that's what it will take, I'll stay down here, crying for another five years! I can do it!

I'm not sure if God shakes His head when we're slow to "get it," but I have honestly pictured Him doing just that while He talked with me. I'm guessing He was realizing that He needed to speed up the conversation because He continued, *Mary, if I don't "fix"* (the children) *in the next 10 years or even until you draw your dying breath, will you continue to cry for the rest of your life?*

WHOA! WHAT?? I was still on the floor, but I'd pulled my elbows up and propped my head in one hand by now. *The rest of my life?!!* I think I was approaching 60. My dad was approaching 90. I had some longevity genes! I began to seriously ponder whether it was possible for me to cry for another thirty years!

That was when my Lord began to explain things to me. Once again, these were not audible words. It was "thought speak," inside my head. But I heard Him.

He said, *Mary, you are My ambassador. How are* (the children) *ever going to know you experience joy in Me if all they ever see you do is cry? Mary, they are good. You're missing the blessings around you.* Then He added, *What have I taught you to do in ALL circumstances?*

Before I could answer, He also added, *Mary, with you there will always be something.*

My mind was racing. I knew He had just asked me a question, and I needed to answer about what to do in all circumstances, but had Jehovah God just told me my children were "good"? Now some of you reading this will wonder why I could have been majorly shocked at that. Were my children drug dealers? Thieves? Alcoholics? No, they were not. Please allow me to leave the scene of me on the floor and take you deep into my brain to explain my shock. I'd grown up reading the Bible. What instantly startled me was that word, "good." I had a distinct recall of Jesus discussing the use of that word with a rich man. (To read the verses yourself, see Matthew 19:16–17, NKJV.) The man had called Jesus "good" and Jesus had explained that none is truly "good" except God. Apparently, Jesus was trying to help His hearers come to grips with the fact that HE and God were one.

But I digress…There I was, on the floor, crying out to God to forgive me and "fix" my children for not being sure they even believed in Him anymore, and HE was DEFENDING them to ME! WHAT?? Then it hit me. If God, my Father, was telling me my children were GOOD, and no one is good except Him, then He had to be telling me HE was INSIDE my children! HIS SPIRIT was in my children! HIS goodness was still INSIDE them. They had asked Him to be their Lord and Savior once, and He hadn't forgotten! HALLELUJAH!! HE called them GOOD!! My spirt began to lift. Oh yes! He had asked me a question. Now I was able to concentrate.

I thought of 1 Thessalonians 5:16–18 and answered, *"I'm to pray without ceasing, rejoice always and give thanks in all circumstances."*

He then asked me if I would do all of that. I sat up and told Him yes. I believe it was six months later that the prophetess (in Mickey Mouse ears at the small group meeting) spoke to me about the disappointment that was still inside me. I had been rejoicing, AND giving thanks, but down deep I STILL *felt* like a failure. After she spoke the word of knowledge over me, I resisted Satan, and he hasn't been able to entrap me since! (Well, not for long periods of time, anyway!)

Here's the truth: I am a failure. That's why I need Jesus. I've asked HIM to be the King of my life, and I've removed myself from sitting on the throne of my pride. Furthermore, HE tells me that I'm precious to HIM. I'm not full of worth because of what I have or haven't done. I'm precious because HE says I am. Here is my version of John 3:16: For God so loved me that He sent His Son, Jesus, who was more than willing to come to planet Earth to pay the penalty—to DIE—for all of my wrongs, so that if I will believe in the death and Resurrection of Jesus and put my trust in Him, as well as immerse myself in His teachings, I will be saved not only from hell and damnation but also from the myriad of torturous emotions brought by Satan and his demons while I remains on Earth and forever. Those words, of course, are NOT what you read in your Bible. But it's what the verse means to me!

My children have all gone on to marry and have children of their own. They're responsible, loving parents. Two of them still seem to be trying to keep their distance from the Lord, but life ain't over, and I'm still praying that the blinders will be removed, their eyes and ears will be opened, and they'll EXPERIENCE the Lord—with joy!!

Here's the point of my sharing my struggles: heart aches come to each of us. Whether it's the pandemic, the death of a family member, a chronic illness, the emptiness of our cupboards, or rejection by those we love, heartache comes.

What do we do with it?

We could get angry. We could take it out on those around us and make everyone miserable. OR we can humbly approach Jehovah God, King of Kings and Lord of Lords, and ask Him for help. He's our Creator, our Sustainer, our Helper, our Good Shepherd, and our Rock. Will He "fix" this Coronavirus pandemic? I don't know. He hasn't told me what He plans to do about the virus. He DOES, however, continue to work on ME! It seems like perhaps I would be wise to ask myself if I am doing my part. (Or maybe He's the One asking): Am I rejoicing even though we're all in quarantine? Am I trusting HIM? Am I sharing and expressing a joy-filled-heart to those around me?

Here's what I know: He loves me and He's with me each and every day. He'll comfort me and give me good ideas for facing whatever lies ahead. I'm not alone. His Word is true. I can read the Bible and depend on It! His fruits are bountiful: Love, joy, peace, patience, kindness, goodness, faithfulness, gentleness and self-control (Galatians 5:22–23). No matter WHAT nor how deep the heartache, if we've asked Jesus to be our Savior, and surrendered ourselves to Him and His will for us, we WILL experience His presence and joy in Him always. What did Jesus, Himself, tell His disciples just before He ascended to heaven—after His resurrection? We read:

Jesus came and told his disciples, "I have been given all authority in heaven and on earth. Therefore, go and make disciples of all the nations, baptizing them in the name of the Father and the Son and the Holy Spirit. Teach these new disciples to obey all the commands I have given you. And be sure of this: I am with you always, even to the end of the age" (Matthew 28:18–20).

I am a disciple (or student) of Jesus. I was baptized into the name of the Father and the Son (Jesus) and the Holy Spirit. Therefore, the promise Jesus made as stated above, is for ME!! He is with me always! Furthermore, He said ALL authority in heaven and on Earth has been given to Him. He knows everything!! That's not only a marvelous spiritual blessing, it's an enormously practical blessing as well!

Yesterday I was getting ready to virtually assist one of my granddaughters who, like the majority of U.S. children, is confined to her house and is now being homeschooled. Her parents both work from home on their computers all day, so my son had asked if my husband and I could assist with her schooling.

I knew I had purchased math flash cards for young children within the past year for some tutoring I do at the local, public school. But, where were they? I started looking in the logical places, but when I didn't find them in my first two searches, I simply prayed, "Lord, will you please help me find those cards? I know that You know where they are!" I continued to walk through the house, looking inside and outside of areas where my grandchildren typically play, when I looked on the top of a low-lying bookcase. Right there, on top of the bookcase sat a boxless stack of math flashcards. HOORAY! Full set?? It didn't matter. I thanked my Father and had to smile at my "find" as I walked to get a book from the children's bookcase in another room. What was this? Two more of those flashcards simply lying on one of the shelves. Then, hearing something accidentally hit the floor, I looked down and saw ANOTHER flashcard! Precious Lord. Such a little, inconsequential matter to the rest of the world, but He loves me and He's concerned about the things I'm concerned about—little or not.

So, He had communicated to me—He led me to the flashcards. Flashcards! Busy with Coronavirus, hospitals, frightened people, politicians, and on and on, and yet, He let me know there was still NOTHING that was too inconsequential to Him where I'm concerned. That's one of the zillion reasons I love Him and can depend on Him. He cares for me!

Another curious thing that happened during the time we spent in quarantine involved, of all things, dinosaurs! David and I have long known we enjoy working together on jigsaw puzzles. We had put together all of the "adult" puzzles we had on hand, and David had even ordered more for us. But, there was a "lag" time between ordering and receiving one batch of puzzles. So, I went through the puzzles I kept on hand for the grandchildren. Sure enough, I found two puzzles that contained 100 pieces. They wouldn't be much of a challenge, but enough for some fun for a few minutes. So, we started. It was a picture of a family of pigs on an outing. Where were they headed? It took me a minute and a magnifying glass to see the picture on the arch through which they were about to walk. It was a picture of a dinosaur. Was the pig family about to enter a park full of dinosaurs?

Suddenly, a scene began to appear in my brain. It was of a host of children coming out of being cooped up and coming into MY yard to look for dinosaurs. LIGHTBULB!! I could see it all. I knew what to do. I went upstairs and started going through the toy boxes we kept for our grandchildren. DINOSAURS!! Not many, and not very large, but they'd do. I told my husband, and he agreed. In fact, he asked if he could put an "announcement" on our neighborhood website. The announcement was posted, the dinosaurs went outside, and the children came.

We hid the dinosaurs in the trees, in the bushes, in a flower pot and on the sidewalk. Seven dinosaurs and one fire-breathing dragon. And the little children loved looking for and finding them. It gave the parents someplace to take the children for a few minutes for an adventure. David ended up ordering twelve more, so the herd grew and the dinosaurs moved around, and the children returned. It has been great fun to hear the laughter in our front yard.

Why do I share this story? Because I believe GOD gave me the idea! My Father loves little children! He CREATED them! He wanted them to have fun. He wanted David and me to get to hear the laughter of those precious children in our yard. We haven't been able to get with our own grandchildren, and God wanted to brighten OUR days! He's sweet and kind and good! Little things mean a LOT to Him. We mean a lot to Him. You mean a lot to Him. He's been trying to get your attention.

Brothers and sisters, in the scripture passage we read several pages ago, we read about God ENCOURAGING US to SEEK HIS FACE!! (2

Chronicles 7:14). He welcomes our FACE TO FACE greeting and communication. OUR GOD WANTS intimate communication with US!! He wants us to experience HIS joy! HIS Love! HIS peace! I have a distinct memory of hearing a young woman, who'd gone to church all her life, upon suddenly realizing what Christianity is really about, exclaiming, "RELATIONSHIP? I had NO IDEA Christianity is about RELATIONSHIP to God!"

The Holy Spirit is READY for contact.

Final Prayer and Exhortation

Holy Father, I pray we will all be receptive to Your communications to us, primarily through your Holy Scripture, but also, through any means You choose, whenever You choose to communicate with us. I also pray, with all my heart, that the world will become aware of Your graciously compassionate care for each of us! I pray we will say we're sorry for any time we've rejected you and your Word. I pray we will all—including myself—whether we intended to or not—stop quenching Your Spiritual nudges. I pray this in the precious and most holy name of Jesus Christ, my Lord and Savior, Amen.

Dear reader, please know that He loves each of His children more than any of us can fathom—enough to leave Heaven, come to Earth as a baby, live here for 33 years, and go through the most grueling death imaginable.

He said He stands at the door and knocks. (Revelation 3:20) He's waiting for you to answer. If you haven't already done so, please invite Him into your life. Surrender control of your life to Him. He is able. Jesus said HE is THE Way, THE Truth and THE Life (John 14:6). If you are new to His love or have walked with Him a while, be prepared to experience afresh His amazing love—and life-giving *Communication from God* for yourself.

Because HE Lives,

Mary Lynn Tao

*See Proclamation on the next page:

PROCLAMATION

BY THE GOVERNOR

WHEREAS, the people of Tennessee are thankful to call this remarkable state home, from the towering Smoky Mountains in the east to the mighty Mississippi River in the west, and every remarkable scene in between; for our people who come from all over the world to find opportunity and hope in our thriving cities and beautiful rural communities; for this and much more we give thanks; and

WHEREAS, we seek forgiveness from our transgressions; from acts of discrimination, oppression, and injustice; and inaction caused by greed, pride, and indifference; for these and many more we ask forgiveness; and

WHEREAS, the people of Tennessee seek wisdom and discernment for our state in the days ahead to support thriving families and communities across our state, to promote an environment of opportunity for every Tennessean, and to ensure our safety and freedom; for these challenges we seek wisdom; and

WHEREAS, the people of Tennessee acknowledge our rich blessings, our deep transgressions, and our complex challenges, and further acknowledge the need to give thanks to God Almighty, to turn from our transgressions and ask for God's forgiveness, and to humble ourselves and seek God's wisdom and guidance;

NOW, THEREFORE, I, Bill Lee, Governor of the State of Tennessee, do hereby proclaim October 10, 2019 as a voluntary

Day of Prayer, Humility, and Fasting

in Tennessee and encourage all citizens to join me in this worthy observance.

IN WITNESS WHEREOF, I have hereunto set my hand and caused the official seal of the State of Tennessee to be affixed at Nashville on this fourth day of October, 2019.

_____
Governor

_____
Secretary of State

ABOUT THE AUTHOR

Mary Lynn Tao has been writing stories of her answered prayers for many years. As a frequent speaker at ladies' retreats throughout the Northeast in the 1980s and 90s, she regularly incorporated stories of God's faithfulness in her talks. The women seemed to love hearing the stories and encouraged her to write a book.

For a number of years, she wrote weekly Bible lessons for the women behind bars when she took part in prison ministry in Pennsylvania.

Over her lifetime, she has taught every age of Bible class from babies using songs and hand motions, through teaching adults using Bible studies.

She has written and directed children's plays and, along with her husband, David, a Christian musical for adults entitled, *A Touch of Seasoning*. Mary also wrote the lyrics and melodies for a dozen songs to encourage mothers of small children. David provided the harmonies and instrumentation needed to record the songs on an album called *More Than Just.*

Mary is wife to David and mother of four. Her four children have blessed her with seven grandchildren. She delights in singing silly songs to them and making up and telling them stories—often about a pig named Jeffrey.

Mary's greatest delight is in sharing God's Word with anyone who will listen. She loved telling Bible stories to her children and now to her grandchildren. She prays that this book, *Communication from God*, will outlive her and encourage her children and their children—along with anyone else who reads it—for generations to come.

Mary and David make their home outside of Nashville, Tennessee. Write to Mary Lynn Tao at COMMUNICATIONFROMGOD@gmail.com.

ACKNOWLEDGEMENTS

First of all, I want to thank my Lord, Jesus, in His total three-in-ONE dimension, for having remained a constant encourager to me all these years. In Him all things are possible.

Then I thank my precious mother, who not only encouraged me in my walk with my Lord, but who also walked me to His gathering house week after week, month after month, year after year, decade after decade. Her love for Jesus blessed all her children, her family, and her community. Her influence and encouragement are with me always. I thank my dad, too, whose dogged endurance in the face of hardship and difficulty inspire me to this day. His sense of humor and conscious mispronunciation of words infected me and, I'm glad to say, as I've passed his antics along—they have delighted my children and grandchildren as well.

Next I must thank my dear husband, David, who has seen me through it all. I started this book a few years into his 35 year career and am now finishing it when he's retired. He has supported me all the way. Thank you, Dear One.

Then I thank my children who were, unconsciously, my teachers along the way. The Holy Spirit used my mistakes in mothering, as well as my impatience and selfishness as a human being, to teach, stretch and, I admit it, to humble me. I needed it all. Still do! I'm not the woman today that I was when I first cradled each of you in my arms. Thank God! I learned from you all. I'm still learning. Thank you.

Next I thank the multitude of Bible class teachers I had along the way. Men and women. I particularly recall Mrs. Scattergood, who gave me the best advice she could have: "Never take what I or your parents or anyone says for fact. You go to the Bible and if you find it there, you'll know it's true." I thank God for those words!!

Finally, I thank all of the friends and family who have prayed for me and this book over the years. Various ones have shouldered the load from time to time. Bud and Eva were champions for a while. Steady encouragers. Many have added their voices of support along the way: I'm thankful for each of my siblings who may not have known they were praying for the book, but they prayed (and one continues to pray) for me, and I cherish those prayers. Also thank you to Kim, Karen, Linda, Jeana, Jack, Joanne, Patti and Bob, Maurine and Buddy, Kathy, Cathy, Donna and Yong, Sally, Susan, Wendy, Lona and all the members of Heartprint Writers' Group. God sent me to you! I also want to thank Kayla and Loral and Seth of Selah Press Publishing. Such blessings!

I thank all the women from my Moms in Touch group in Pennsylvania and the members of my Moms in Prayer group in Tennessee. Prayer warriors all! I couldn't forget Ricki and Tina's Care Group—MANY thanks, dear friends!! And then there's Pam, John, and Emma. Emma used her artistic gifting to create the cover. I also would like to thank all those who ever encouraged me to write. I could go on and on. And maybe I should. But I'll stop. My Heavenly Father knows each and every one of you who has played a part in my writing journey over the years. May He encourage each of you mightily—and may you HEAR HIM!!

Because HE Lives,

Mary

Mary

NOTES

1. Cambridge Dictionary, s.v., "in (prep.)," accessed April 9, 2020, https://dictionary.cambridge.org/dictionary/english/in.

2. Merriam-Webster, s.v. "stifle (v.)," accessed April 9, 2020, https://www.merriam-webster.com/dictionary/stifle.

3. Merriam-Webster, s.v. "quench (v.)," accessed April 10, 2020, https://www.merriam-webster.com/dictionary/quench.

Made in the USA
Coppell, TX
19 July 2021